Apache Mahout Clustering Designs

Explore the clustering algorithms used with
Apache Mahout

Ashish Gupta

PUBLISHING

BIRMINGHAM - MUMBAI

Apache Mahout Clustering Designs

First published: September 2015

Production reference: 1240915

Published by Packt Publishing Ltd.
Livery Place
35 Livery Street
Birmingham B3 2PB, UK.

ISBN 978-1-78328-443-6

www.packtpub.com

Credits

Author
Ashish Gupta

Reviewers
Siva Prakash

Tharindu Rusira

Commissioning Editor
Akram Hussain

Acquisition Editors
Vivek Anantharaman

Divya Poojari

Content Development Editor
Susmita Sabat

Technical Editor
Namrata Patil

Copy Editor
Merilyn Pereira

Project Coordinator
Judie Jose

Proofreader
Safis Editng

Indexer
Rekha Nair

Graphics
Abhinash Sahu

Production Coordinator
Manu Joseph

Cover Work
Manu Joseph

About the Author

Ashish Gupta has been working in the field of software development for the last 10 years. He has worked in companies such as SAP Labs and Caterpillar as a software developer. While working for a start-up predicting potential customers for new fashion apparels using social media, he developed an interest in the field of machine learning. Since then, he has worked on big data technologies and machine learning for different industries, including retail, finance, insurance, and so on. He is passionate about learning new technologies and sharing that knowledge with others. He is the author of the book, *Learning Apache Mahout Classification, Packt Publishing*. He has organized many boot camps for Apache Mahout and the Hadoop ecosystem.

First of all, I would like to thank the open source communities for their continuous efforts in developing great software. I would also like to thank the reviewers of this book.

Nothing can be accomplished without the support of family, friends, and loved ones; I would like to thank them, especially my wife and son, for their continuous support while writing this book.

About the Reviewers

Siva Prakash has been working in the field of software development for the last 7 years. He is currently working in CISCO, Bangalore. He has extensive development experience in desktop, mobile, and web-based applications in ERP, telecom, and the digital media industry. He is passionate about learning new technologies and sharing knowledge with others. He has worked on big data technologies for the digital media industry. He loves trekking, traveling, music, reading books, and blogging.

He is available on LinkedIn at https://www.linkedin.com/in/techsivam.

Tharindu Rusira is currently working as a graduate research assistant at the School of Computing, University of Utah while pursuing his doctoral studies in computer science, specializing in compiler technology for performance optimization. He is also passionate about machine learning and its applications in a wide spectrum of real-world problems.

Tharindu is available on LinkedIn at https://www.linkedin.com/in/trusira.

www.PacktPub.com

Support files, eBooks, discount offers, and more

For support files and downloads related to your book, please visit www.PacktPub.com.

Did you know that Packt offers eBook versions of every book published, with PDF and ePub files available? You can upgrade to the eBook version at www.PacktPub.com and as a print book customer, you are entitled to a discount on the eBook copy. Get in touch with us at service@packtpub.com for more details.

At www.PacktPub.com, you can also read a collection of free technical articles, sign up for a range of free newsletters and receive exclusive discounts and offers on Packt books and eBooks.

https://www2.packtpub.com/books/subscription/packtlib

Do you need instant solutions to your IT questions? PacktLib is Packt's online digital book library. Here, you can search, access, and read Packt's entire library of books.

Why subscribe?

- Fully searchable across every book published by Packt
- Copy and paste, print, and bookmark content
- On demand and accessible via a web browser

Free access for Packt account holders

If you have an account with Packt at www.PacktPub.com, you can use this to access PacktLib today and view 9 entirely free books. Simply use your login credentials for immediate access.

Table of Contents

Preface

With the progress in hardware, our storage capacity has increased now, and because of this, there are many organizations that want to store all types of events for analytical purpose. This is giving birth to a new area of machine learning. The field of machine learning is very complex, and writing those algorithms is not a piece of cake. Apache Mahout provides us with readymade algorithms in the area of machine learning and saves us from the complex task of algorithm implementation.

The intention of this book is to cover clustering algorithms available in Apache Mahout. Whether you have already worked on clustering algorithms using some other tool, or whether you are completely new to this field, this book will help you. So, start reading this book, explore the clustering algorithms in a strong, community-supported, open source, and one of the most popular Apache projects—Apache Mahout.

What this book covers

Chapter 1, *Understanding Clustering*, explains clustering in general. This chapter will further discuss the different distance matrices and how to calculate them.

Chapter 2, *Understanding K-means Clustering*, introduces K-means clustering and how Mahout can be used for K-means clustering algorithms.

Chapter 3, *Understanding Canopy Clustering*, introduces Canopy clustering and its uses in Apache Mahout.

Chapter 4, *Understanding the Fuzzy K-means Algorithm Using Mahout*, talks about the Fuzzy K-means algorithm and how this algorithm works as a preprocessing step for K-means. We will further discuss how to use Mahout for the Fuzzy K-means algorithm.

Chapter 5, Understanding Model-based Clustering, discusses model-based clustering. This chapter further discusses the topic of modeling using Dirichlet clustering.

Chapter 6, Understanding Streaming K-means, introduces the Streaming K-means algorithm, which is used for streaming data. We will further discuss how Mahout can be used for Streaming K-means.

Chapter 7, Spectral Clustering, introduces spectral clustering and how Mahout has implemented spectral clustering.

Chapter 8, Improving Cluster Quality, covers the steps that should be followed to improve cluster quality once you are ready with your clustering algorithm, in detail. It also discusses what techniques Mahout provides to improve cluster quality.

Chapter 9, Creating a Cluster Model for Production, introduces the techniques that should be followed in a production environment while applying the clustering algorithm.

What you need for this book

To use the examples in this book, you should have the following software installed in your system:

- Java 1.6 or further
- Eclipse
- Hadoop
- Mahout (we will discuss the installation in *Chapter 2, Understanding K-means Clustering*)
- Maven (depending on how you are installing Mahout)

Who this book is for

If you are a data scientist who has some experience with the Hadoop ecosystem and machine learning methods and want to try out clustering on large datasets using Mahout, this book is ideal for you. Knowledge of Java is essential.

Conventions

In this book, you will find a number of text styles that distinguish between different kinds of information. Here are some examples of these styles and an explanation of their meaning.

Code words in text, database table names, folder names, filenames, file extensions, pathnames, dummy URLs, user input, and Twitter handles are shown as follows: "Once done, you can test it by typing the command – mahout and this will show you the same screen as shown in preceding figure."

A block of code is set as follows:

```
generateSamples(500, 1, 1, 3); // 500 samples of sd 3
generateSamples(300, 1, 0, 0.5); //300 sample of sd 0.5
generateSamples(300, 0, 2, 0.1); //300 sample of sd 0.1
```

Any command-line input or output is written as follows:

```
bin/mahoutcanopy --input /user/hue/20newsdatavec/tfidf-
vectors/ --output /user/hue/canopycentroids --distanceMeasure
org.apache.mahout.common.distance.EuclideanDistanceMeasure -t1
1550  --t2 2050--method mapreduce
```

New terms and **important words** are shown in bold. Words that you see on the screen, for example, in menus or dialog boxes, appear in the text like this: "Click on the **Keys and Access Tokens** tab, and you will find **ConsumerKey** and **ConsumerSecret** under **Application Settings**."

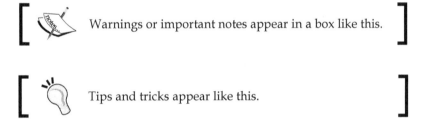

> Warnings or important notes appear in a box like this.

> Tips and tricks appear like this.

Reader feedback

Feedback from our readers is always welcome. Let us know what you think about this book—what you liked or disliked. Reader feedback is important for us as it helps us develop titles that you will really get the most out of.

To send us general feedback, simply e-mail feedback@packtpub.com, and mention the book's title in the subject of your message.

If there is a topic that you have expertise in and you are interested in either writing or contributing to a book, see our author guide at www.packtpub.com/authors.

Customer support

Now that you are the proud owner of a Packt book, we have a number of things to help you to get the most from your purchase.

Downloading the example code

You can download the example code files from your account at `http://www.packtpub.com` for all the Packt Publishing books you have purchased. If you purchased this book elsewhere, you can visit `http://www.packtpub.com/support` and register to have the files e-mailed directly to you.

Errata

Although we have taken every care to ensure the accuracy of our content, mistakes do happen. If you find a mistake in one of our books—maybe a mistake in the text or the code—we would be grateful if you could report this to us. By doing so, you can save other readers from frustration and help us improve subsequent versions of this book. If you find any errata, please report them by visiting `http://www.packtpub.com/submit-errata`, selecting your book, clicking on the **Errata Submission Form** link, and entering the details of your errata. Once your errata are verified, your submission will be accepted and the errata will be uploaded to our website or added to any list of existing errata under the Errata section of that title.

To view the previously submitted errata, go to `https://www.packtpub.com/books/content/support` and enter the name of the book in the search field. The required information will appear under the **Errata** section.

Piracy

Piracy of copyrighted material on the Internet is an ongoing problem across all media. At Packt, we take the protection of our copyright and licenses very seriously. If you come across any illegal copies of our works in any form on the Internet, please provide us with the location address or website name immediately so that we can pursue a remedy.

Please contact us at `copyright@packtpub.com` with a link to the suspected pirated material.

We appreciate your help in protecting our authors and our ability to bring you valuable content.

Questions

If you have a problem with any aspect of this book, you can contact us at questions@packtpub.com, and we will do our best to address the problem.

1
Understanding Clustering

Reduced hardware cost is giving us the opportunity to save a lot of data. We are now generating a lot of data, and this data can generate interesting patterns for various industries, which is why machine learning and data mining enthusiasts are responsible for this data.

The data from various industries can provide insights that can be very useful for the business. For example, sensor data on cars can be very useful for insurance majors. Data scientists can find out useful information from this data, such as driving speed, time of driving, mileage, breaking, and so on; they can also rate the driver, which in turn would be useful for the insurer to set up the premium.

In the health care industry, data collected from different patients is used to predict different diseases. A well-known use case is to predict whether a tumor will be cancerous or not based on the tumor size and other characteristics.

In bioinformatics, one well-known use case is grouping a homologous sequence into the gene family.

These problems are related to data gathering, finding useful pattern from data, and then enabling the machine to learn to identify patterns from new datasets. In the area of machine learning, learning can broadly be classified into the following three areas:

- **Supervised learning**: In supervised learning, each sample consists of the input and the desired output, and we tried to predict the output from the given input set
- **Unsupervised learning**: In unsupervised learning, we do not know anything about the output, but from the pattern of data, we can define different collections within the datasets
- **Reinforcement learning**: In reinforcement learning, within a given context, machines and software agents automatically determine the ideal behavior

In this book, we will concentrate on unsupervised learning and the different methods applied to this. For the tool perspective, we will use Apache Mahout. You will learn what the algorithms available in Apache Mahout in the area of unsupervised learning are and how to use them.

In this chapter, we will explore following topics:

- Understanding clustering
- Applications of clustering
- Understanding distance measures
- Understanding different clustering techniques
- Algorithm support in Apache Mahout
- Installing Apache Mahout
- Preparing data for use by clustering techniques

The clustering concept

Since childhood, we have been grouping similar things together. You can see that kids demand something (such as candies, ice cream, chocolates, toys, a cycle, and so on) in return for a favor. We can see examples in our organizations where we group people (peers, vendors, clients, and so on) based on their work.

The idea of clustering is similar to this. It is a technique that tries to group items together based on some sort of similarity. These groups will be divided in a way that the items in one group have little or no similarity to the items in a different group.

Let's take an example. Suppose you have a folder in your computer that is filled with videos and you know nothing about the content of the videos. One of your friends asks you whether you have the science class lecture video. What will you do in this case? One way is to quickly check the content of the videos, and as soon as you find the relevant video you will share it. Another way of doing this is to create a subfolder inside your main folder and categorize the videos by movies, songs, education, and so on. You can further organize movies as action, romance, thriller, and so on. If you think again, you have actually solved one of your clustering problems—grouping similar items together in such a way that they are similar in one group but different from the other group.

Now, let's address a major question that beginners usually ask at this stage—how is it is different from classification? Take your video folder example again; in the case of classification, subfolders of movies, songs, and education will already be there, and based on the content, you will put your new videos into relevant folders. However, in the case of clustering, we were not aware of the folders (or labels in machine learning terms) based on the content, we divided the videos and later assigned the label to them.

As you can see in the following figure, we have different points and based on shapes, we group them into different clusters:

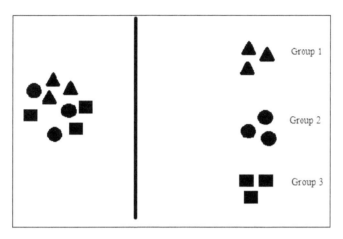

The clustering task can be divided into the following:

- **The pattern finding algorithm**: We will discuss these algorithms throughout this book; they are K-means, spectral clustering, and so on. The basic idea is that we should have an algorithm that can detect patterns in given datasets.

- **The distance measuring technique**: To calculate the closeness of different items, there are certain measures in place, such as Euclidean distance, cosine distance measure, and so on. We will discuss different techniques of distance measure in this chapter.

- **Grouping and Stopping**: With the algorithm and distance measure techniques, items will be grouped in different clusters, and based on the conditions, such as the elbow method, cross validation, and so on, we will stop further grouping.

- **Analysis of Output**: Once grouping is complete, we have a measuring technique to determine how well our model performed. We can use techniques such as F-measure, the Jaccard index, and so on to evaluate the cluster. We will discuss these techniques with the respective algorithm discussions.

Application of clustering

Clustering is used in a wide area of applications such as bioinformatics, web search, image pattern recognition, and sequence analysis. There are a number of fields where clustering is used. Some of them are as follows:

- **For marketing**: Clustering can be useful to segment customers based on geographical location, age, and consumption patterns. Clustering can be used to create a 360 degree view of customers, which is useful for customer relationship management. This is useful in creating new customers, retaining existing customers, launching new products, and in product positioning.

- **For recommendations**: Clusters are very useful in creating recommendation system applications. Recommender systems are applications that suggest new items to customers based on their previous search or based on the item purchased by similar customers. Clustering is useful to create groups of customers based on their preferences.

- **Image segmentation**: Clustering is used to partition the image into multiple regions and pixel in each region shares the common properties.

- **In bioinformatics**: Clustering is used in many areas of bio-informatics and one major area is human genome clustering—identifying patterns in a genome, which leads to discover the cure for disease.

- **Clustering in web search**: Clustering is useful to group results, resulted after keyword search on the Web.

Clustering is useful in almost all industries, and clustering is studied and researched in different areas such as data mining, machine learning, statistics, databases, biology, astrophysics, and many other fields.

Now, we will move on to the next section where we will discuss the different distance measuring technique that we used to find the similarity, or dissimilarity, between two data points as numeric values.

Understanding distance measures

In each clustering problem, such as document clustering, protein clustering, genome sequence, galaxy image grouping, and so on, we need to calculate the distance between points. Let's start this problem with the points in a two-dimensional XY plane, and later in the section of preparing data for Mahout, we will discuss how to handle other types of documents, such as text.

Suppose that we have a set of points and know the points' coordinates (x and y position). We want to group the points into different clusters. How do we achieve this? For this type of problem, we will calculate the distance between points, the points close to each other will be part of one cluster, and the points; that are away from one group will be part of another. See the following figure:

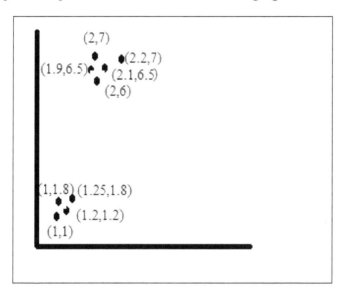

Any clustering algorithm will divide the given points into two groups, and with great accuracy, but, to be honest, in a real scenario, we will not face such simple problems. As defined, we used a distance measure to calculate the distance between points. We will only discuss distance measuring techniques that are available in the Apache Mahout 0.9 releases. An introduction of Mahout is given later in this chapter. For numeric variables, distance measures are as follow:

- ChebyshevDistanceMeasure

- CosineDistanceMeasure

- EuclideanDistanceMeasure

- MahalanobisDistanceMeasure

- ManhattanDistanceMeasure

- MinkowskiDistanceMeasure

- SquaredEuclideanDistanceMeasure

- TanimotoDistanceMeasure

- `WeightedEuclideanDistanceMeasure`
- `WeightedManhattanDistanceMeasure`

Note that for categorical variables, distance is measured with matching categories. For example, say we have six categories of variables, three type of colors, and two sets of data:

	Color 1	Color 2	Color 3	Color 4	Color 5	Color 6
Dataset 1	Blue	Red	Green	Red	Blue	Blue
Dataset 2	Red	Red	Green	Blue	Green	Green

We can see that we have two matching and four nonmatching items, so the distance will be 4/6 ~= 0.67.

Let's understand what these distance measures are, but, before that, here's a reminder about the vectors that you learn in your physics class. A vector is a quantity that has both magnitude and direction. As shown in the figure, we represent a vector on the Cartesian plane by showing coordinates.

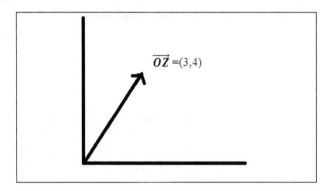

$\overrightarrow{OZ} = (3,4)$

`EuclideanDistanceMeasure` is the simplest among all the distance measures. Euclidean distance between two n-dimensional vectors $(x_1, x_2, x_3...x_n)$ and $(y_1, y_2, y_3...y_n)$ is calculated as summing the square root of the squared differences between each coordinate. Mathematically, it is represented as:

$$Euclidean\ Distance = \sqrt{(x_1 - y_1)^2 + (x_2 - y_2)^2 + \cdots (x_n - y_n)^2}$$

The Mahout implementation of the Euclidean distance is available as the `EuclideanDistanceMeasure` class under the `org.apache.mahout.common.distance` package.

`SquaredEuclideanDistanceMeasure` is the square of the Euclidean distance. It provides greater weights to points that are farther apart. It is implemented as the `SquaredEuclideanDistanceMeasure` class under the `org.apache.mahout.common.distance` package. Mathematically, it is represented as:

$$Squared\ Euclidean\ Distance = (x_1 - y_1)^2 + (x_2 - y_2)^2 + \cdots (x_n - y_n)^2$$

`WeightedEuclideanDistanceMeasure` is implemented as the `WeightedEuclideanDistanceMeasure` class under the `org.apache.mahout.common.distance` package. In Weighted Euclidean Distance, squared differences between the variables are multiplied by their corresponding weights. Weights can be defined as:

$Wi = \dfrac{1}{s_i}^{\frac{1}{s_i}}$ where s_i is sample standard deviation of *ith* variable.

Mathematically, Weighted Euclidean Distance is represented as:

$$Weighted\ Euclidean\ Distance = \sqrt{w_1(x_1 - y_1)^2 + w_2(x_2 - y_2)^2 + \cdots w_n(x_n - y_n)^2}$$

`ManhattanDistanceMeasure` is the sum of absolute difference between the coordinates. It is implemented as the `ManhattanDistanceMeasure` class under the same package, as other distance measure classes exist. Manhattan distance is also called taxicab geometry. It is based on grid-like street geography of Manhattan, New York. In this grid structure, distance is the sum of horizontal and vertical lines. As shown in the following figure, the Manhattan distance for point A and B from line 1 and 2 is equal to 9 blocks:

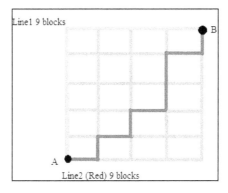

Mathematically, this is defined as:

$$Manhattan\ distance = \left|\left(x_1 - y_1\right)\right| + \left|\left(x_2 - y_2\right)\right| \ldots + \left|\left(x_n - y_n\right)\right|$$

The `WeightedManhattanDistanceMeasure` class is implemented as `WeightedManhattanDistanceMeasure` under the same distance package in Mahout. This class implements a Manhattan distance metric by summing the absolute values of the difference between each coordinate with weights, as in case of weighted Euclidean distance.

The `ChebyshevDistanceMeasure` distance measure is equivalent to a maximum of the absolute value of the difference between each coordinate. This distance is also known as chessboard distance because of the moves a king can make. Mathematically, this can be defined as:

$$Chebyshev\ distance = \max\left(\left|x_1 - y_1\right|, \left|x_2 - y_2\right| \ldots ., \left|x_n - y_n\right|\right)$$

So, let's say, for example, that we have two vectors, vector X *(0,2,3,-4)* and vector Y *(6,5,4,1)*. The Chebyshev distance will be maximum (|0-6|,|2-5|,|3-4|,|-4-1|), which is 6.

This class is defined as `ChebyshevDistanceMeasure` under the same distance package in Mahout.

The `CosineDistanceMeasure` Cosine distance is a little different from the distance measures that we have studied so far. Cosine distance measures the similarity of the two vectors as the measure of the cosine of the angle between two vectors. Consider the following figure for more clarity. We have two vectors A and B, and the angle between them is θ.

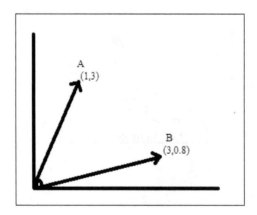

Cosine of the angle will be close to 1 for a smaller angle and decreases for a larger angle. Cosine for 90^0 is 0 and cosine for 180^0 is -1. So, vectors in the same directions have a similarity of 1, and those in the opposite direction have a similarity of -1. Mathematically, it is defined as:

$$Cosine\,Distance = 1 - \frac{\left(x_1 y_1 + x_2 y_2 + \cdots + x_n y_n\right)}{\sqrt{\left(x_1^2 + x_2^2 .. x_n^2\right)}\sqrt{\left(y_1^2 + y_2^2 .. y_n^2\right)}}$$

Subtraction of 1 is used to provide a proper distance so vectors close to each other (0^0) will provide 0, and those opposite each other (180^0) will provide 2. So, in this distance, instead of the vector length, their directions matters.

`MinkowskiDistanceMeasure` is a generalization of the Euclidean and Manhattan distance. This distance is defined in the `MinkowskiDistanceMeasure` class under the same distance package of Mahout. Mathematically, it is defined as:

$$Minkowski\,Distance = \left(\sum_{i=1}^{n}\left|x_i - y_i\right|^c\right)^{1/c}$$

If you see, for *c=1*, it is the Manhattan distance measure, and for *c=2*, it is the Euclidean distance measure.

`TanimotoDistanceMeasure`: In cosine distance, we take only the angle between the vectors into account but for the tanimoto distance measure, we also take the relative distance of vectors into account. Mathematically, it can be defined as:

$$Tanimoto\,Distance = 1 - \frac{\left(x_1 y_1 + x_2 y_2 + \cdots + x_n y_n\right)}{\sqrt{\left(x_1^2 + x_2^2 .. x_n^2\right)} + \sqrt{\left(y_1^2 + y_2^2 .. y_n^2\right)} - \left(x_1 y_1 + x_2 y_2 + \cdots + x_n y_n\right)}$$

This is defined as the `TanimotoDistanceMeasure` class under the `org.apache.mahout.common.distance` package.

Understanding different clustering techniques

A number of different clustering techniques are available in the area of machine learning and data mining. There are algorithms based on these different techniques. Let's see these different techniques:

Hierarchical methods

In this clustering method, the given data is divided hierarchically. To help you understand this, let's take an example of animals' class hierarchy. We have two groups, invertebrate and vertebrate, but we can combine them into one animal class. Hierarchical clustering can be done using two approaches, which are:

- **The top-down approach**: This is also called the divisive approach. In this approach, all the datasets start with one cluster, and each iteration cluster is further divided into sub clusters. This process goes on until we meet a termination condition.

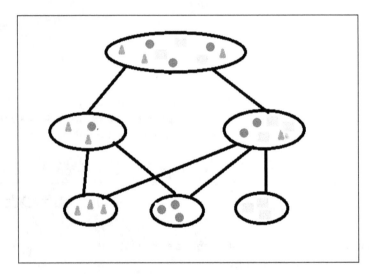

- **The bottom-up approach**: This approach is also called the agglomerative approach. This method starts with each dataset in separate clusters and successively merges the dataset into closer clusters until all sub clusters are merged into one cluster.

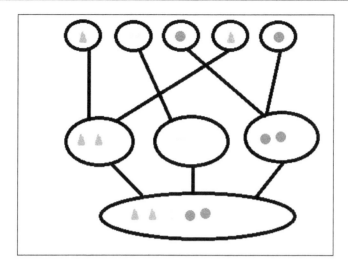

We can take a real-life example from our organizational structure. We have all the employees' data, and we can divide them into clusters such as finance, HR, operations, and so on. The main pain point of hierarchical clustering is deciding between merger or split points.

The partitioning method

In this method, we select a number, k, to create k numbers of clusters. Partitioning methods are generally distance-based.

The partitioning method involves a few steps to acquire better partitioning. First, it creates the initial partitioning, and after that, it calculates the similarity of items based on the distance measuring techniques. Iteratively, it relocates the objects to another group based on the similarity it calculates. Partitioning is said to be good if it keeps similar items in one cluster while the items in different clusters are different from each other.

K-means is a very good example of this method. K-means is used in many areas, such as human genetic clustering, shopping cart item clustering, and so on. We will discuss these algorithms in the upcoming chapter.

The density-based method

The density-based clustering algorithm groups together points that are closely packed together. So, for each data point within a given cluster, the neighborhood of a given radius has to contain at least a minimum number of points, which is given as part of the input to the algorithm. Such a method can be used to filter out noise or outliers. DBSCAN is a very popular algorithm in this area. It can detect arbitrary shapes in the cluster, and it can detect outliers in the data. This should not be used for high-dimensional datasets.

Probabilistic clustering

In probabilistic clustering, we take up the problems where we know that data is coming from different models of probability distribution. The probabilistic clustering algorithm takes a probabilistic model and tries to fit the data into that model.

The model that we built is used to fit the given dataset. The model is said to be right if it fits the data better and shows the number of clusters in the given dataset in line with the model.

By calculating the probability of the model being a fit for dataset and reading the vectors, we test whether a dataset is a fit for the model. This is also called soft clustering.

Algorithm support in Mahout

The implementation of algorithms in Mahout can be categorized into two groups:

- **Sequential algorithms**: These algorithms are executed sequentially and so cannot use Hadoop's scalable processing. These algorithms are usually the ones derived from Taste (this was a separate project. It was a non Hadoop based recommendation engine).

  Examples of these algorithms are user-based collaborative filtering, logistic regression, Hidden Markov Model, multi-layer perceptron, and singular value decomposition.

- **Parallel algorithms**: These algorithms can support petabytes of data using Hadoop's map reduce parallel processing.

  Examples of these algorithms are Random Forest, Naïve Bayes, Canopy clustering, K-means clustering, spectral clustering, and so on.

Clustering algorithms in Mahout

Mahout has the implementation of the following clustering algorithms (as of release 0.9):

- **K-means clustering**: This is available as both single machine and map reduce way

- **Fuzzy K-means**: This is available as both single machine and map reduce way

- **Streaming K-means**: This is available as both single machine and map reduce way

- **Spectral clustering**: This is available only as map reduce way

- **Canopy clustering**: This is available as map reduce way

- **Latent Dirichlet Allocation for topic modeling**: This is available as both single machine and map reduce way

Installing Mahout

We can install Mahout using different methods. Each method is independent from the others. You can choose any one of these:

- Building Mahout code using Maven.
- Setting up the development environment using Eclipse
- Setting up Mahout for Windows users

Before performing any of the steps, the prerequisites are:

- Having Java installed on your system
- Having Hadoop installed on your system (`http://hadoop.apache.org/docs/stable/hadoop-project-dist/hadoop-common/SingleNodeSetup.html`)

Building Mahout code using Maven

The Mahout build and release system is based on Maven. For Maven installation:

1. Create the folder `/usr/local/maven`:

```
mkdir /usr/local/maven
```

2. Download the distribution `apache-maven-x.y.z-bin.tar.gz` from the Maven site (`http://maven.apache.org/download.cgi`), and move this to `/usr/local/maven`:

```
mvapache-maven-x.y.z-bin.tar.gz /usr/local/maven
```

3. Unpack this to the location `/usr/local/maven`:

```
tar -xvfapache-maven-x.y.z-bin.tar.gz
```

4. Edit the `.bashrc` file as follows:

```
export M2_HOME=/usr/local/apache-maven-x.y.z
export M2=$M2_HOME/bin
export PATH=$M2:$PATH
```

 For the Eclipse IDE, go to help and select **Install new Software**, click on the add button, and in the popup fill up the name M2Eclipse and provide the `http://download.eclipse.org/technology/m2e/releases` link, and click on **OK**.

Building the Mahout code:

By default, Mahout assumes that Hadoop is already installed on the system. Mahout uses the `HADOOP_HOME` and `HADOOP_CONF_DIR` environment variables to access Hadoop cluster configurations. To set up Mahout, follow the steps given here:

1. Download the Mahout distribution file `mahout-distribution-0.9-src.tar.gz` from `http://archive.apache.org/dist/mahout/0.9/`.

2. Choose an installation directory for Mahout (`/usr/local/Mahout`) and place the downloaded source in the folder. Extract the source code and ensure that the folder contains the `pom.xml` file:

```
tar -xvf mahout-distribution-0.9-src.tar.gz
```

3. Install the Mahout Maven project and skip the test cases during installation:

```
mvn install -Dmaven.test.skip=true
```

4. Set the `MAHOUT_HOME` environment variable in the `~/.bashrc` file and update the `PATH` variable with the Mahout `bin` directory:

```
export MAHOUT_HOME=/user/local/mahout/mahout-distribution-0.9
export PATH=$PATH:$MAHOUT_HOME/bin
```

5. To test the Mahout installation, execute the `mahout` command. This will list the available programs within the distribution bundle, as shown in following screenshot:

```
MAHOUT_LOCAL is not set; adding HADOOP_CONF_DIR to classpath.
Running on hadoop, using /usr/lib/hadoop/bin/hadoop and HADOOP_CONF_DIR=/etc/hadoop/conf
MAHOUT-JOB: /usr/lib/mahout/mahout-examples-0.9.0.2.1.1.0-385-job.jar
An example program must be given as the first argument.
Valid program names are:
  arff.vector: : Generate Vectors from an ARFF file or directory
  baumwelch: : Baum-Welch algorithm for unsupervised HMM training
  canopy: : Canopy clustering
  cat: : Print a file or resource as the logistic regression models would see it
  cleansvd: : Cleanup and verification of SVD output
  clusterdump: : Dump cluster output to text
  clusterpp: : Groups Clustering Output In Clusters
  cmdump: : Dump confusion matrix in HTML or text formats
  concatmatrices: : Concatenates 2 matrices of same cardinality into a single matrix
  cvb: : LDA via Collapsed Variation Bayes (0th deriv. approx)
  cvb0_local: : LDA via Collapsed Variation Bayes, in memory locally.
  evaluateFactorization: : compute RMSE and MAE of a rating matrix factorization against probes
  fkmeans: : Fuzzy K-means clustering
  hmmpredict: : Generate random sequence of observations by given HMM
  itemsimilarity: : Compute the item-item-similarities for item-based collaborative filtering
  kmeans: : K-means clustering
  lucene.vector: : Generate Vectors from a Lucene index
  lucene2seq: : Generate Text SequenceFiles from a Lucene index
  matrixdump: : Dump matrix in CSV format
  matrixmult: : Take the product of two matrices
  parallelALS: : ALS-WR factorization of a rating matrix
  qualcluster: : Runs clustering experiments and summarizes results in a CSV
  recommendfactorized: : Compute recommendations using the factorization of a rating matrix
  recommenditembased: : Compute recommendations using item-based collaborative filtering
  regexconverter: : Convert text files on a per line basis based on regular expressions
  resplit: : Splits a set of SequenceFiles into a number of equal splits
  rowid: : Map SequenceFile<Text,VectorWritable> to {SequenceFile<IntWritable,VectorWritable>, SequenceF
  rowsimilarity: : Compute the pairwise similarities of the rows of a matrix
  runAdaptiveLogistic: : Score new production data using a probably trained and validated Adaptivelogist
  runlogistic: : Run a logistic regression model against CSV data
  seq2encoded: : Encoded Sparse Vector generation from Text sequence files
  seq2sparse: : Sparse Vector generation from Text sequence files
  seqdirectory: : Generate sequence files (of Text) from a directory
  seqdumper: : Generic Sequence File dumper
  seqmailarchives: : Creates SequenceFile from a directory containing gzipped mail archives
  seqwiki: : Wikipedia xml dump to sequence file
  spectralkmeans: : Spectral k-means clustering
```

Setting up the development environment using Eclipse

For this setup, you should have Maven installed on the system and the Maven plugin for Eclipse. Refer to the Installing Maven steps mentioned in a previous section.

1. Download the Mahout distribution file `mahout-distribution-0.9-src.tar.gz` from the `http://archive.apache.org/dist/mahout/0.9/` location and unzip this:

   ```
   tarxzfmahout-distribution-0.9-src.tar.gz
   ```

2. Create a folder name workspace under `/usr/local/workspace`:

    `mkdir /usr/local/workspace`

3. Move the downloaded distribution to this folder (from the downloads folder):

    `mvmahout-distribution-0.9 /usr/local/workspace/`

4. Move to the `/usr/local/workspace/mahout-distribution-0.9` folder and make the Eclipse project:

    `mvneclipse:eclipse` (this command can take up to one hour)

5. Set the Mahout home in the `.bashrc` file, as explained earlier.

6. Now, open Eclipse, select the file and click on import. Under Maven, select **Existing Maven Projects**. Now, browse to the location for `mahout-distribution-0.9` and click on **Finish**.

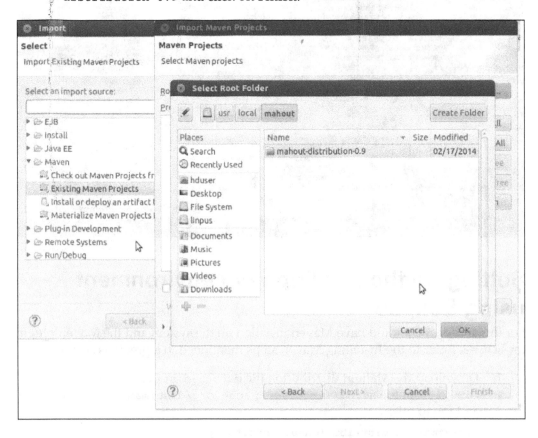

Setting up Mahout for Windows users

Windows users can use `cygwin` to setup their environment. There is one more easy-to-use way.

Download Hortonworks Sandbox for VirtualBox on your system (`http://hortonworks.com/products/hortonworks-sandbox/#install`). On your system, this will be a pseudo-distributed mode of Hadoop. Log in to the console, and enter the following command:

```
yum install mahout
```

Now, you will see the following screen:

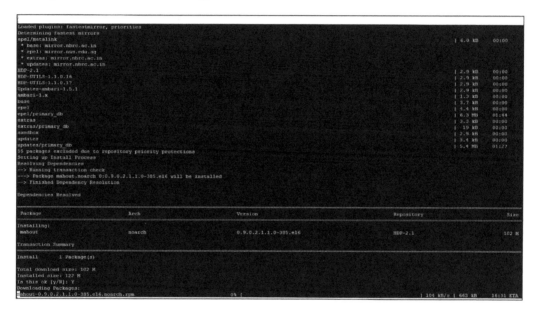

Enter `y` and your Mahout will start installing. Once done, you can test it by typing the command – `mahout`, and this will show you the same screen as shown in preceding figure.

Preparing data for use with clustering techniques

Machine learning algorithms such as clustering and classification use input data in vector formats. We need to map features of an object in the numeric form, which will be helpful in creating the vectors. The vector space model is used to vectorize text documents. Let's understand this model in more detail.

In this model, first we will create a dictionary of all the words present in the document in such a way that we assign a particular index to each word. As some of the words will occur more frequently in any document, such as a, as, the, that, this, was, and so on. These words are also called stop words and will not help us, so we will ignore these words. Now, we have a dictionary of the words that are indexed. So, let's assume that we have two documents, Doc1 and Doc2, containing the following content:

- **Doc1**: We will learn clustering in this book
- **Doc2**: We have different clustering algorithms

Now, we will have the following index dictionary:

[learn , cluster, book, different, algorithm]

[1,2,3,4,5]

So, we have created a vector space of the document, where the first term is learn, the second is cluster, and so on. Now, we will use the term-frequency to represent each term in our vector space. The term-frequency is nothing but the count of how many times the words present in our dictionary are present in the documents. So, each of the Doc1 and Doc2 can be presented by five-dimensional vectors as [1,1,1,0,0] and [0,1,0,1,1] (the number of times each word in particular index occurred in the Doc).

When we try to find the similarity between the documents based on distance measures, we often encounter a problem. Most occurring words in the documents increase the weight. We can find out that two documents could be same if they are talking about the same topic, and for the same topic, words are usually rare and occur less often occurring words. So, to give more weightage for these words, there is a technique that is called **Inverse document frequency**.

Inverse document frequency can be considered as the boost a term gets for being rare. A term should not be too common. If a term is occurring in every document, it is not good for clustering. The fewer documents in which a term occurs, the more significant it is likely to be in the documents it does occur in.

For a term t inverse document frequency is calculated as:

IDF (t) = 1 + log (total number of documents/ number of documents containing t)

Usually, **TF-IDF** is the widely used improvement to provide weightage to words. It is the product of the term frequency and inverse document frequency.

*TFIDF (t, d) = TF (t, d) * IDF (t)*

Where *t* is the term, *d* id the document, *TF(t,d)* is frequency of term t in document *d* and *IDF(t)*, as explained earlier.

Sometimes, we find that some words can be found in groups and make more sense instead of appearing alone. A group of words in a sequence is called **n-grams**. Words that have a high probability to occur together can be identified by Mahout. To find out whether two words occur together by chance or because they are a unit, Mahout passes these n-grams through log-likelihood tests.

Mahout provides two types of implementation of the vector format—sparse vector and dense vector. Applications that require fast random reads use RandomAccessSparseVector, which is a sparse implementation. Applications that require fast sequential reads can use SequentialAccessSparseVector.

Mahout uses sequence files to read and write the vectors. These sequence files are used by Hadoop for parallel execution. A sequence file contains binary key value pairs. Mahout provides commands to convert text document corpse into sequence files and later to generate vectors from those sequence files. These vectors are used as inputs for the algorithms.

Summary

In this chapter, we discussed clustering. We discussed clustering in general, as well as the different applications of clustering. We further discussed the different distance measuring techniques available. We then saw the different clustering techniques and algorithms available in Apache Mahout. We also saw how to install Mahout on the system and how to prepare a development environment to execute Mahout algorithms. We also discussed how to prepare data using Mahout's clustering algorithms.

Now, we will move on to the next chapter, where we will see one of the best known clustering algorithms—K-means. You will learn about the algorithm and understand how to use the Mahout implementation of this algorithm.

2
Understanding K-means Clustering

In the previous chapter, we discussed clustering and the different types of clustering in general. In this chapter, we will discuss one of the most popular algorithms in clustering, K-means. We will discuss the following topics in this chapter:

- Learning K-means
- Using Mahout to execute K-means
- Visualizing the K-means cluster using Mahout

Learning K-means

As you cannot do engineering without math, in the same way, you cannot start a clustering discussion without K-means. This is one of the basic and most useful algorithms.

The name of the algorithm is K-means because by using this, we divide the set of data into K-different clusters. So, this algorithm puts a hard limitation on the number of clusters formed. K-means algorithms follow these steps:

1. The algorithm will start with the selection of the number of clusters — K.
2. It will initialize the K centroid points in the cluster.

3. Now, the closest points of each centroid are computed.

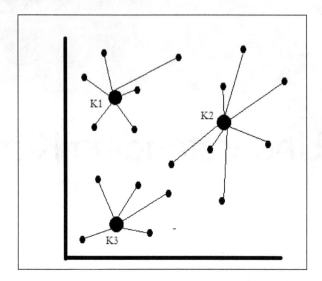

4. Next, the centroid location is recomputed for each cluster.

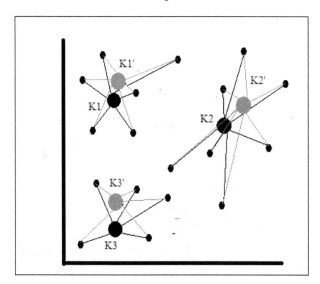

5. Steps 3 and 4 are repeated until the convergence is reached.

Convergence is reached when the location of centroids does not move from one iteration to the next. In an algorithm, we also provide a convergence threshold, which indicates that the centroid does not move more than this distance, and if it is reached, we stop the algorithm.

The K-means algorithm is an example of the **Expectation Maximization (EM)** algorithm.

- **Expectation Step**: We find associated points to a cluster
- **Maximization Step**: In this step, the cluster is improved by calculating the new centroid from the points defined in the first point

The main point for the success of this algorithm is selecting the number of clusters. A wrong selection will result in poor output. One way of selection of K is trying a different number of K based on the data and measuring the resulting sum of the square. Popular techniques for finding K, as defined in different literature, are:

- **The Elbow method**: In this method, a graph is plotted between percentages of variance and the number of clusters. We stop choosing the number of clusters once it stops adding a marginal gap invariance. This creates an elbow in the graph. How to do this calculation is out of scope of this book.

- **The Silhouette coefficient**: To calculate this, first select a random value for k and calculate the distance between a point and all other points in that cluster, calculate the average, and do this for each point in the cluster. This is called the cohesion. Now, do this exercise for each point in the cluster with each point in another cluster. This is called the separation. For a particular point, the Silhouette coefficient is the difference between the separation, and cohesion divided by the maximum of separation and cohesion.

In this way, we can calculate the average coefficient. The maximum silhouette coefficient for a given number of clusters is the choice for the cluster.

Another technique for finding K is at `http://www.ijarcsms.com/docs/paper/volume1/issue6/V1I6-0015.pdf`.

After finding K, the other issue is to find optimal initialization of centroid points. There are algorithms for that, such as Canopy clustering and Fuzzy K-means clustering, which we will discuss later in this book.

Running K-means on Mahout

K-means on mahout runs on the map reduce mode. It uses the Hadoop filesystem to run the algorithm simultaneously. The Mahout algorithm accepts the files written in the sequence file format. Sequence files are binary key-value pairs. K-means runs in the map reduce mode as per the following steps:

In the Map Phase:

- It reads the initial centroids in the memory. These centroids are written in a sequence file.
- Iterates over each input key value pair and measures the distance.
- Writes the vectors along with an assigned center (as the key) to the filesystem.

In the Reducer Phase:

- Iterates over each vector and calculate the average vector.
- This is the new center, and it saves to a sequence file.
- Distance is calculated between an old and new center, and convergence is calculated.
- If convergence is not reached, the counter is updated in Hadoop and the whole iteration is done again.

For the literature perspective, you can have a look at `http://www.cs.ucsb.edu/~veronika/MAE/parallelkmeansmapreduce_zhao.pdf`.

Now, we will use the mahout implementation to run the K-means algorithm, but before that, we have the selection of the dataset.

Dataset selection

We will use the 20 newsgroups dataset for this exercise. The 20 newsgroups dataset is a standard dataset commonly used for machine learning research. The data is from transcripts of several months of postings made in 20 Usenet newsgroups from the early 1990s. The 20 newsgroups dataset consists of messages, one per file. Each file begins with header lines that specify things such as who sent the message, how long it is, what kind of software was used, and the subject. A blank line follows, and then the message body follows as unformatted text.

Download the dataset `20news-bydate.tar.gz` from `http://qwone.com/~jason/20Newsgroups/`.

Executing K-means

The following steps are used to run the Mahout K-means clustering:

1. Create a directory `20newsdata` and unzip the data here:

   ```
   mkdir /tmp/20newsdata
   cd tmp/20newsdata
   tar-xzvf /tmp/20news-bydate.tar.gz
   ```

2. There are two folders under `20newsdata`, `20news-bydate-test` and `20news-bydate-train`. Now, create another directory `20newsdataall` and merge both training and test data of the group.

3. Now, move to the home directory and execute following command:

   ```
   mkdir /tmp/20newsdataall
   cd -R /20newsdata/*/* /tmp/20newsdataall
   ```

4. Create a directory in Hadoop and save this data in HDFS.

   ```
   hadoop fs -mkdir /usr/hue/20newsdata
   hadoop fs -put /tmp/20newsdataall /usr/hue/20newsdata
   ```

5. Mahout will accept data in the vector format. For this, first, we will generate the sequence file from the directory:

   ```
   bin/mahout seqdirectory -i /user/hue/20newsdata/20newsdataall
   -o /user/hue/20newsdataseq-out
   ```

```
mahout seqdirectory -i /user/hue/20newsdata/20newsdataall -o /user/hue/20newsdataseq-out
MAHOUT_LOCAL is not set; adding HADOOP_CONF_DIR to classpath.
Running on hadoop, using /usr/lib/hadoop/bin/hadoop and HADOOP_CONF_DIR=/etc/hadoop/conf
MAHOUT-JOB: /usr/lib/mahout/mahout-examples-0.9.0.2.1.1.0-385-job.jar
14/11/01 09:33:07 INFO common.AbstractJob: Command line arguments: {--charset=[UTF-8], --chunkSize=[64], --endPhase=[2147483647], --fileFilterClass=
ext.PrefixAdditionFilter], --input=[/user/hue/20newsdata/20newsdataall], --keyPrefix=[], --method=[mapreduce], --output=[/user/hue/20newsdataseq-out
--tempDir=[temp]}
14/11/01 09:33:08 INFO Configuration.deprecation: mapred.input.dir is deprecated. Instead, use mapreduce.input.fileinputformat.inputdir
14/11/01 09:33:08 INFO Configuration.deprecation: mapred.compress.map.output is deprecated. Instead, use mapreduce.map.output.compress
14/11/01 09:33:08 INFO Configuration.deprecation: mapred.output.dir is deprecated. Instead, use mapreduce.output.fileoutputformat.outputdir
14/11/01 09:33:12 INFO client.RMProxy: Connecting to ResourceManager at sandbox.hortonworks.com/10.0.2.15:8050
14/11/01 09:33:22 INFO input.FileInputFormat: Total input paths to process : 18846
14/11/01 09:33:24 INFO input.CombineFileInputFormat: DEBUG: Terminated node allocation with : CompletedNodes: 1, size left: 35855003
14/11/01 09:33:25 INFO mapreduce.JobSubmitter: number of splits:1
14/11/01 09:33:25 INFO mapreduce.JobSubmitter: Submitting tokens for job: job_1414852457629_0001
14/11/01 09:33:27 INFO impl.YarnClientImpl: Submitted application application_1414852457629_0001
14/11/01 09:33:27 INFO mapreduce.Job: The url to track the job: http://sandbox.hortonworks.com:8088/proxy/application_1414852457629_0001/
14/11/01 09:33:27 INFO mapreduce.Job: Running job: job_1414852457629_0001
14/11/01 09:34:01 INFO mapreduce.Job: Job job_1414852457629_0001 running in uber mode : false
14/11/01 09:34:01 INFO mapreduce.Job:  map 0% reduce 0%
14/11/01 09:34:30 INFO mapreduce.Job:  map 1% reduce 0%
```

6. Convert the sequence file into a sparse vector:

   ```
   bin/mahout seq2sparse -i /user/hue/20newsdataseq-out/part-m-
   00000 -o /user/hue/20newsdatavec -lnorm -nv -wt tfidf
   ```

   ○ `-lnorm`: This is for the output vector; it should be log normalized

   ○ `-nv`: This is for the named vector

   ○ `-wt`: The kind of weight to use here is tfidf

7. Now, we will execute the command to the run K-means cluster:

```
bin/mahout kmeans --input /user/hue/20newsdatavec/tfidf-
vectors/ --output /user/hue/Kmeansout --clusters
/user/hue/kmeanscenter --numClusters 10 --distanceMeasure
org.apache.mahout.common.distance.EuclideanDistanceMeasure --
maxIter 20 --method mapreduce --clustering
```

  ○ `--input`: This is the input vector that has a directory

  ○ `--output`: This is the directory for the output

  ○ `--clusters`: This is a file path containing the initial cluster

  ○ `--numClusters`: This is the number of clusters

  ○ `--distanceMeasure`: This is the distance measure used in the algorithm

  ○ `--maxIter`: This is the maximum iteration independent of convergence

  ○ `--method`: This is the mapreduce or sequential

  ○ `--clustering`: This is a Boolean vector to indicate that the Clustering step is to be executed after the cluster is determined

8. The confusing parameter here is clusters. Here, we have mentioned an empty directory path on HDFS for this. The KMeansDriver class that runs the MapReduce version of K-means will use RandomSeedGenerator to randomly specify centroids.

```
[root@sandbox ~]$ mahout kmeans --input /user/hue/20newsdatavec/tfidf-vectors/ --output /user/hue/Kmeansout --clusters /user/hue/kmeanscenter --numClusters 10 --distanc
eMeasure org.apache.mahout.common.distance.EuclideanDistanceMeasure --maxIter 20 --method mapreduce --clustering
MAHOUT_LOCAL is not set; adding HADOOP_CONF_DIR to classpath.
Running on hadoop, using /usr/lib/hadoop/bin/hadoop and HADOOP_CONF_DIR=/etc/hadoop/conf
MAHOUT-JOB: /usr/lib/mahout/mahout-examples-0.9.0.2.1.1.0-385-job.jar
15/03/09 04:21:50 INFO common.AbstractJob: Command line arguments: {--clustering=null, --clusters=[/user/hue/kmeanscenter], --convergenceDelta=[0.5], --distanceMeasure=
[org.apache.mahout.common.distance.EuclideanDistanceMeasure], --endPhase=[2147483647], --input=[/user/hue/20newsdatavec/tfidf-vectors/], --maxIter=[20], --method=[mapre
duce], --numClusters=[10], --output=[/user/hue/Kmeansout], --startPhase=[0], --tempDir=[temp]}
15/03/09 04:21:55 INFO common.HadoopUtil: Deleting /user/hue/kmeanscenter
15/03/09 04:21:55 INFO zlib.ZlibFactory: Successfully loaded & initialized native-zlib library
15/03/09 04:21:55 INFO compress.CodecPool: Got brand-new compressor [.deflate]
15/03/09 04:21:59 INFO kmeans.RandomSeedGenerator: Wrote 10 Klusters to /user/hue/kmeanscenter/part-randomSeed
15/03/09 04:22:00 INFO kmeans.KMeansDriver: Input: /user/hue/20newsdatavec/tfidf-vectors Clusters In: /user/hue/kmeanscenter/part-randomSeed Out: /user/hue/Kmeansout
15/03/09 04:22:00 INFO kmeans.KMeansDriver: convergence: 0.5 max Iterations: 20
15/03/09 04:22:00 INFO compress.CodecPool: Got brand-new decompressor [.deflate]
15/03/09 04:22:01 INFO client.RMProxy: Connecting to ResourceManager at sandbox.hortonworks.com/10.0.2.15:8050
15/03/09 04:22:08 INFO input.FileInputFormat: Total input paths to process : 1
15/03/09 04:22:08 INFO mapreduce.JobSubmitter: number of splits:1
15/03/09 04:22:09 INFO mapreduce.JobSubmitter: Submitting tokens for job: job_1425884469193_0011
15/03/09 04:22:09 INFO impl.YarnClientImpl: Submitted application application_1425884469193_0011
15/03/09 04:22:09 INFO mapreduce.Job: The url to track the job: http://sandbox.hortonworks.com:8088/proxy/application_1425884469193_0011/
15/03/09 04:22:09 INFO mapreduce.Job: Running job: job_1425884469193_0011
15/03/09 04:22:36 INFO mapreduce.Job: Job job_1425884469193_0011 running in uber mode : false
15/03/09 04:22:36 INFO mapreduce.Job:  map 0% reduce 0%
15/03/09 04:23:23 INFO mapreduce.Job:  map 12% reduce 0%
15/03/09 04:23:26 INFO mapreduce.Job:  map 37% reduce 0%
15/03/09 04:23:29 INFO mapreduce.Job:  map 41% reduce 0%
15/03/09 04:23:32 INFO mapreduce.Job:  map 100% reduce 0%
15/03/09 04:24:01 INFO mapreduce.Job:  map 100% reduce 100%
15/03/09 04:24:07 INFO mapreduce.Job: Job job_1425884469193_0011 completed successfully
15/03/09 04:24:08 INFO mapreduce.Job: Counters: 49
```

9. This command will take some time to complete; once done, you can inspect the output folder using the following command:

    ```
    hadoop fs -ls / user/hue/Kmeansout
    ```

10. This will show the cluster folders and the `clusteredPoint` folder, which is generated as we have used the clustering option in the previous command.

```
Found 23 items
 rw  r   r      1 root  hue         194 2015 03 09 04:18 /user/hue/Kmeansout/_policy
drwxr-xr-x      - root  hue           0 2015-03-09 04:49 /user/hue/Kmeansout/clusteredPoints
drwxr-xr-x      - root  hue           0 2015-03-09 04:22 /user/hue/Kmeansout/clusters-0
drwxr-xr-x      - root  hue           0 2015-03-09 04:24 /user/hue/Kmeansout/clusters-1
drwxr-xr-x      - root  hue           0 2015-03-09 04:37 /user/hue/Kmeansout/clusters-10
drwxr-xr-x      - root  hue           0 2015-03-09 04:38 /user/hue/Kmeansout/clusters-11
drwxr-xr-x      - root  hue           0 2015-03-09 04:39 /user/hue/Kmeansout/clusters-12
drwxr xr x        root  hue           0 2015 03 09 04:41 /user/hue/Kmeansout/clusters 13
drwxr-xr-x      - root  hue           0 2015-03-09 04:42 /user/hue/Kmeansout/clusters-14
drwxr-xr-x      - root  hue           0 2015-03-09 04:43 /user/hue/Kmeansout/clusters-15
drwxr-xr-x      - root  hue           0 2015-03-09 04:44 /user/hue/Kmeansout/clusters-16
drwxr-xr-x      - root  hue           0 2015-03-09 04:46 /user/hue/Kmeansout/clusters-17
drwxr-xr-x      - root  hue           0 2015-03-09 04:47 /user/hue/Kmeansout/clusters-18
drwxr-xr-x      - root  hue           0 2015-03-09 04:48 /user/hue/Kmeansout/clusters-19
drwxr-xr-x      - root  hue           0 2015-03-09 04:25 /user/hue/Kmeansout/clusters-2
drwxr-xr-x      - root  hue           0 2015-03-09 04:48 /user/hue/Kmeansout/clusters-20-final
drwxr-xr-x      - root  hue           0 2015-03-09 04:27 /user/hue/Kmeansout/clusters-3
drwxr-xr-x      - root  hue           0 2015-03-09 04:28 /user/hue/Kmeansout/clusters-4
drwxr-xr-x      - root  hue           0 2015-03-09 04:29 /user/hue/Kmeansout/clusters-5
drwxr-xr-x      - root  hue           0 2015-03-09 04:31 /user/hue/Kmeansout/clusters-6
drwxr-xr-x      - root  hue           0 2015-03-09 04:32 /user/hue/Kmeansout/clusters-7
drwxr-xr-x      - root  hue           0 2015-03-09 04:34 /user/hue/Kmeansout/clusters-8
drwxr-xr-x      - root  hue           0 2015-03-09 04:36 /user/hue/Kmeansout/clusters-9
```

11. We have the cluster output as the sequence file to view the generated output, and we have the `clusterdumper` utility available in Mahout. This will convert the output to a human-readable format. We will execute following command for this:

    ```
    bin/mahoutclusterdump -i /user/hue/Kmeansout/clusters-20-final
    -o /user/hue/clusterdumpout.txt -d
    /user/hue/20newsdatavec/dictionary.file-0 -dt sequencefile --
    pointsDir /user/hue/Kmeansout/clusteredPoints
    ```

    - `-input`: This is the sequence file
    - `-o`: The output file will be generated at local filesystem
    - `-d`: This is the dictionary file location
    - `-dt`: This is the type of directory as sequence file

- ° `-pointsDir`: This is the clustered points' directory that we generate using a Clustering option

```
[root@sandbox ~]# mahout clusterdump -i /user/hue/Kmeansout/clusters-20-final -o /user/hue/clusterdumpout/ -d /user/hue/20newsdatavec/dictionary.file-0 -dt sequencefile
--pointsDir /user/hue/Kmeansout/clusteredPoints
MAHOUT_LOCAL is not set; adding HADOOP_CONF_DIR to classpath.
Running on hadoop, using /usr/lib/hadoop/bin/hadoop and HADOOP_CONF_DIR=/etc/hadoop/conf
MAHOUT-JOB: /usr/lib/mahout/mahout-examples-0.9.0.2.1.1.0-385-job.jar
15/03/09 08:05:35 INFO common.AbstractJob: Command line arguments: [--dictionary=[/user/hue/20newsdatavec/dictionary.file-0], --dictionaryType=[sequencefile], --distanc
eMeasure=[org.apache.mahout.common.distance.SquaredEuclideanDistanceMeasure], --endPhase=[2147483647], --input=[/user/hue/Kmeansout/clusters-20-final], --output=[/user/
hue/clusterdumpout/], --outputFormat=[TEXT], --pointsDir=[/user/hue/Kmeansout/clusteredPoints], --startPhase=[0], --tempDir=[temp]]
15/03/09 08:06:05 INFO clustering.ClusterDumper: Wrote 10 clusters
```

The clusterdump result

Open the `Clusterdump` file using `cat/user/hue/clusterdumpout.txt`:

VL-10510{n=21 c=[0:0.204, 0,0:0.006, 0,1:0.003, 0,2:0.001, 0,3:0.001,….
r=[0:4.885, 01:2.643, 03:6.721,….

Top Terms:

you	=>	4.147502350268882
i	=>	3.8812103205498167
we	=>	3.761726649069734
have	=>	3.567675752354988
he	=>	3.4668349408790826
who	=>	3.3493214848262065
people	=>	3.319086533954173
all	=>	3.168451756955235
what	=>	3.1607294402153756
were	=>	3.1507695170970007

  Weight : [props - optional]: Point:
: [distance=218.125104193978]: /alt.atheism/49960 =

You will see the preceding output, where:

- VL represents a converged cluster, and if you got CL, it means that the convergence is still not reached for that cluster
- n is the number of points in the cluster
- c is the centroid of the cluster
- r is the radius of the cluster

Top Terms are the most occurring terms in the cluster.

Now that you have learned how to run K-means in Mahout, let's move to a small utility available in Mahout to visualize the cluster.

Visualizing clusters

The T Mahout example package provides classes to generate a sample dataset.

For K-means, `DisplayKmeans` is the class that displays the cluster. You can directly run the class. As per the code in the class, points are generated as follows:

```
generateSamples(500, 1, 1, 3); // 500 samples of sd 3
generateSamples(300, 1, 0, 0.5); //300 sample of sd 0.5
generateSamples(300, 0, 2, 0.1); //300 sample of sd 0.1
```

Data is a set of randomly-generated 2D data points, and the points are generated using a normal distribution centered at a mean location with a constant standard deviation.

Once you run this class, you will view the clusters, as shown here:

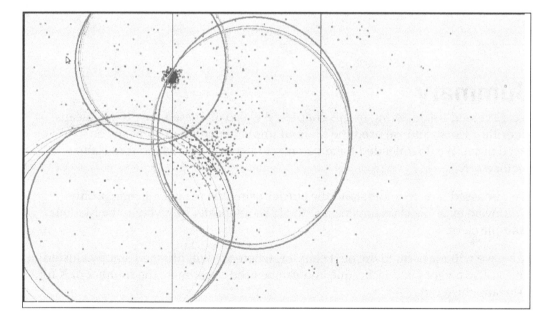

The final clustering done by the algorithm is shown using a bold red colored circle. In the console, you can find the output related to points generation and cluster formation.

Summary

We discussed K-Clustering in this chapter. We also discussed how the K-means algorithm works and we used the Mahout implementation of K-means on a text dataset. We downloaded the data and converted it to a Mahout reusable vector format.

We discussed how to understand the cluster using the `clusterdumper` utility. We saw an example class to visualize the Mahout cluster as given in the Mahout example class.

Now, we will move on to the next chapter, where we will discuss Canopy clustering. This is also a very good technique and can be used to estimate the number of K for K-means clustering.

3
Understanding Canopy Clustering

In the previous chapter, we discussed K-means clustering and used Mahout to run K-means clustering on the text dataset. Therein, we discussed that one of the main challenges is to identify the initial number of clusters. We discussed the different techniques that we can use to identify the number of clusters in the dataset. One such technique is Canopy clustering. This algorithm is also called the preclustering algorithm. In this chapter, we will discuss Canopy clustering in detail. We will cover the following topics:

- Learning Canopy clustering
- Using Mahout to execute Canopy clustering
- Visualizing Canopy cluster using Mahout
- Working with CSV files

Canopy clustering, which is a pre-clustering algorithm, is used to estimate the approximate number of clusters in the dataset, as well as approximate centroids for those clusters. Canopy in Canopy cluster refers to the enclosure that has points. It is a very fast algorithm and runs without the initial set of clusters. Canopy clustering runs as follows:

1. The algorithm uses dataset points in the vector format and two threshold values, T1 and T2. (T1>T2).
2. It selects a point from the dataset and starts a new Canopy.
3. It calculates the distance from the selected point to other points in the dataset, and if the distance is less than T2, points will be removed from the dataset and will not be part of the new Canopy.

4. Points that are between the T1 and T2 distances are also part of this Canopy but are allowed to be part of another Canopy too.

5. Step 2 and onwards is repeated until there are no more points in the dataset.

A data point can be part of many Canopies. This algorithm is not good for high-dimensional data. High-dimensional data will be part of many Canopies that will lead to confusing results.

Now that we know how Canopy clustering works in general, one question that arises is: how to select the initial thresholds? Generally, for the small dataset, one approach is to find out the distance between all the points and you can then get an idea of the distance range for the points. Now, accordingly, we can select the threshold points. As we are working with Mahout, obviously, our dataset is very huge. For huge datasets, random sample do the job. We can take different random samples from the dataset and can get the range of distances that, in turn, gives us an estimated idea of the thresholds.

Running Canopy clustering on Mahout

Canopy clustering on mahout runs on Hadoop's MapReduce mode. The algorithm is implemented using the map reduce steps. It uses the Hadoop sequence file format as an input. The steps are as follows:

1. Convert the data into a form that you can use as an input. This is called data messaging.

2. As per the input set received, each mapper runs Canopy clustering and outputs its Canopy centers.

3. Reducers received the Canopy center and clusters these centers to produce the final Canopy center.

4. Data points are assigned to these Canopies.

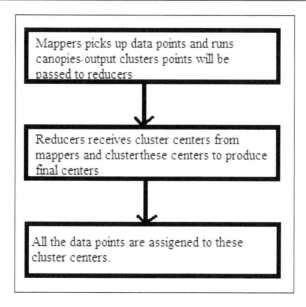

The whole process we are referring to can be understood using the Canopy generation phase and the Canopy clustering phase. The process is available at `https://mahout.apache.org/users/clustering/canopy-clustering.html`

The Canopy generation phase

During the map step, each mapper processes a subset of the total points and applies the chosen distance measure and thresholds to generate Canopies. In the mapper, each point that is found to be within an existing Canopy will be added to an internal list of Canopies. After observing all its input vectors, the mapper updates all of its Canopies and normalizes their totals to produce Canopy centroids, which are output, using a constant key (centroid) to a single reducer. The reducer receives all of the initial centroids and, again, applies the Canopy measure and thresholds to produce a final set of Canopy centroids, which is the output (that is, clustering the cluster centroids). The reducer output format is Sequence File (Text, Canopy), with the key encoding the Canopy identifier.

The Canopy clustering phase

During the clustering phase, each mapper reads the Canopies produced by the first phase.

Since all mappers have the same Canopy definitions, their outputs will be combined during the shuffle so that each reducer (many are allowed here) will see all of the points assigned to one or more canopies. The output format will then be SequenceFile (IntWritable, WeightedVectorWritable) with the key encoding the Canopy ID. The WeightedVectorWritable has two fields—a double weight and a VectorWritable vector. Together, they encode the probability that each vector is a member of the given Canopy.

We will use the same 20newsgroups dataset that we used in our previous chapter.

Running Canopy clustering

The following steps are used to run Mahout Canopy clustering:

1. We will execute the command to run Canopy cluster:

   ```
   bin/mahoutcanopy --input /user/hue/20newsdatavec/tfidf-
   vectors/ --output /user/hue/canopycentroids --distanceMeasure
   org.apache.mahout.common.distance.EuclideanDistanceMeasure -t1
   1550  --t2 2050--method mapreduce
   ```

   ◦ --input: This is the input vector that has a directory

   ◦ --output: This is the output file path containing the clusters

   ◦ --distanceMeasure: This is the distance measure used in the algorithm

   ◦ --method: This is mapreduce or sequential

   ◦ --t1: This is threshold T1

   ◦ --t2: This is threshold T2

```
[root@sandbox ~]# mahout canopy --input /user/hue/20newsdatavec/tfidf-vectors/ --output /use
r/hue/canopycentroids --distanceMeasure org.apache.mahout.common.distance.EuclideanDistanceM
easure -t1 1550 --t2 2050 --method mapreduce
MAHOUT_LOCAL is not set; adding HADOOP_CONF_DIR to classpath.
Running on hadoop, using /usr/lib/hadoop/bin/hadoop and HADOOP_CONF_DIR=/etc/hadoop/conf
MAHOUT-JOB: /usr/lib/mahout/mahout-examples-0.9.0.2.1.1.0-385-job.jar
15/03/21 06:45:39 INFO common.AbstractJob: Command line arguments: {--distanceMeasure=[org.a
pache.mahout.common.distance.EuclideanDistanceMeasure], --endPhase=[2147483647], --input=[/u
ser/hue/20newsdatavec/tfidf-vectors/], --method=[mapreduce], --output=[/user/hue/canopycentr
oids], --startPhase=[0], --t1=[1550], --t2=[2050], --tempDir=[temp]}
15/03/21 06:45:39 INFO canopy.CanopyDriver: Build Clusters Input: /user/hue/20newsdatavec/tf
idf-vectors Out: /user/hue/canopycentroids Measure: org.apache.mahout.common.distance.Euclid
eanDistanceMeasure@3b3edaee t1: 1550.0 t2: 2050.0
15/03/21 06:45:43 INFO client.RMProxy: Connecting to ResourceManager at sandbox.hortonworks.
com/10.0.2.15:8050
15/03/21 06:46:00 INFO input.FileInputFormat: Total input paths to process : 1
15/03/21 06:46:01 INFO mapreduce.JobSubmitter: number of splits:1
15/03/21 06:46:02 INFO mapreduce.JobSubmitter: Submitting tokens for job: job_1426943617672_
0001
15/03/21 06:46:03 INFO impl.YarnClientImpl: Submitted application application_1426943617672_
0001
15/03/21 06:46:04 INFO mapreduce.Job: The url to track the job: http://sandbox.hortonworks.c
om:8088/proxy/application_1426943617672_0001/
15/03/21 06:46:04 INFO mapreduce.Job: Running job: job_1426943617672_0001
15/03/21 06:46:50 INFO mapreduce.Job: Job job_1426943617672_0001 running in uber mode : fals
e
15/03/21 06:46:50 INFO mapreduce.Job:  map 0% reduce 0%
15/03/21 06:47:25 INFO mapreduce.Job:  map 100% reduce 0%
15/03/21 06:47:51 INFO mapreduce.Job:  map 100% reduce 100%
15/03/21 06:47:54 INFO mapreduce.Job: Job job_1426943617672_0001 completed successfully
15/03/21 06:47:55 INFO mapreduce.Job: Counters: 49
        File System Counters
              FILE: Number of bytes read=1012675
```

2. Check the cluster output directory and you will find a directory containing the sequence file that has a cluster identifier and Canopy.

Using the Canopy output for K-means

Since we have generated the initial set of clusters using Canopy clustering, we can use this initial set of clusters to run the K-means algorithm. We will use the following command to run K-means clustering:

```
bin/mahout kmeans --input /user/hue/20newsdatavec/tfidf-vectors/ --
output /user/hue/Kmeansout --clusters user/hue/canopycentroids
/clusters-0-final --distanceMeasure
org.apache.mahout.common.distance.EuclideanDistanceMeasure --maxIter
20 --method mapreduce --clustering
```

Now, run this command and notice the change in the output. I am leaving this as an exercise for you.

Visualizing clusters

Mahout under the `mahout-example` package provides the classes to generate a sample dataset. In this class, it runs the reference clustering implementations over them.

For Canopy, `DisplayCanopy` is the class that displays the cluster. You can directly run the class. As per the code in the class, points are generated as follows:

```
generateSamples(500, 1, 1, 3); // 500 samples of sd 3
generateSamples(300, 1, 0, 0.5); //300 sample of sd 0.5
generateSamples(300, 0, 2, 0.1); //300 sample of sd 0.1
```

Once you run this class, you will view the clusters as shown here:

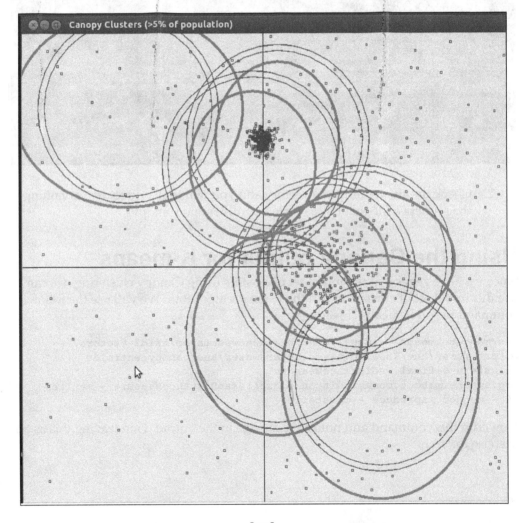

The bold red color is the final clustering done by the algorithm. In the console, you can find the output related to the generation of points and cluster formation.

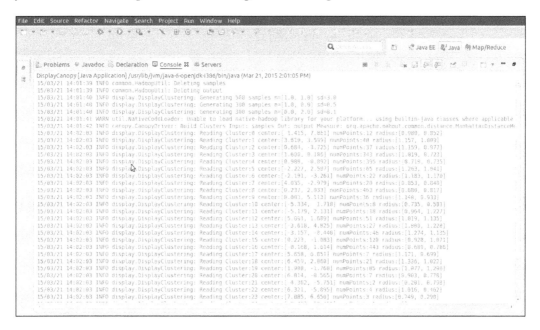

Working with CSV files

Generally, a problem that arises while using Mahout algorithms is how to use files that are in CSV, TSV, or in a similar format. So, here, again, the main challenge is to convert the files into vector format. Once done, the rest of the process is the same as defined previously. Let's look at the code that takes a CSV file and writes the vector format that is usable by Mahout:

```
public String getSeqFile(String inputLocation) throws Exception {
    String outputPath="<output path>"; //Location where you want to
save the output
    FileSystem fs = null;
    SequenceFile.Writer writer;
    fs = FileSystem.get(getConfiguration());
    Path vecoutput =new Path(outputPath);
    writer = new SequenceFile.Writer(fs, getConfiguration(),
      vecoutput, Text.class, VectorWritable.class);
    VectorWritable vec = new VectorWritable();
      try {
//File reader takes input location as an input.
```

```
            FileReader fr = new FileReader(inputLocation);
            BufferedReader br = new BufferedReader(fr);
            String s = null;
            String key = "Key";
            while((s=br.readLine())!=null){
//File Separator could be '/t',',','|' etc.
                String spl[] = s.split(getFileSperator());
                Integer val = 0;
                for(int i=1;k<spl.length;i++){

                    colvalues[val] = Double.parseDouble(spl[i]);
                        val++;
                }
//Named vector with the values stores as dense vector
            NamedVector nmv = new NamedVector(new
                DenseVector(colvalues),key);
            vec.set(nmv);
            writer.append(new Text(nmv.getName()), vec);


            }



            writer.close();


        }
        catch (Exception e) {
          System.out.println("ERROR: "+e);
        }
//Return the output path
        return outputPath;
    }


    //A method for configuration setup.
    private Configuration getConfiguration() {
      Configuration conf = new Configuration();
      conf.addResource(new Path("/etc/hadoop/conf/core-site.xml"));
      conf.addResource(new Path("/etc/hadoop/conf/hdfs-site.xml"));
      conf.addResource(new Path("/etc/hadoop/conf/yarn-site.xml"));
      return conf;
    }
```

Using these two methods you can convert your CSV files into vector format, which is used by Mahout.

Here, we assume that our CSV file contains numeric data. If you have text data as a field in CSV, first convert that to an appropriate numeric value before using the preceding code.

This method can be modified to use CSV, TSV, or a pipe separated file.

Summary

We discussed Canopy clustering in this chapter and found out how to get the initial number of clusters using Canopy clustering. We discussed how the Canopy clustering algorithm works and used the Mahout implementation of Canopy on a text dataset to generate Canopies. We discussed how Canopy clustering is implemented using the MapReduce method. We saw an example class to visualize the Mahout cluster as given in the mahout example class. We also discussed the code to change the CSV file to the vector format that is used by Mahout.

Now, we will move on to the next chapter, where we will discuss the Fuzzy K-means clustering algorithm. This is also a very good topic under clustering algorithms.

4
Understanding the Fuzzy K-means Algorithm Using Mahout

In the previous chapter, we discussed Canopy clustering and used Mahout to run Canopy clustering. In this chapter, we will discuss a new algorithm in clustering—Fuzzy K-means. Fuzzy clustering is also called soft clustering because data points can belongs to more than one cluster. Fuzzy K-means clustering is also called **Fuzzy C-Means (FCM)**. We will discuss the following topics in this chapter:

- Learning Fuzzy K-means clustering
- Using mahout to execute Fuzzy K-means clustering
- Visualizing the Fuzzy K-means cluster using Mahout

Learning Fuzzy K-means clustering

Fuzzy K-means clustering is a fuzzy form of the K-means algorithm that we discussed earlier. Fuzzy K-means generate soft clusters, in which a point can belong to more than one cluster and will have a valid affinity in that cluster. Fuzzy K-means is helpful in defining the relationship between the different data points. It is good for clustering text documents. This algorithm takes similar parameters as K-means, except for one additional fuzziness factor. Fuzzy K-means iterates over the dataset and calculates a degree of association of each point to each of the clusters. So, the degree of association happens in this way—suppose that we have centroids c_1, c_2, and c_3, and we have distances $d1$, $d2$, and $d3$ for a vector V from centroids c_1, c_2, and c_3.

The degree of association for centroid c1 will be calculated as:

$$\frac{1}{\sum_{i=1}^{k}\left(\dfrac{d1}{di}\right)^{\frac{2}{m-1}}}$$

Here, k is the number of centroids and m is the fuzziness factor. In the same way, we can calculate the degree of association with other centroids after changing the value of $d1$ to $d2$, $d3$, ...dk. The value for m will always be greater than 1; otherwise, the equation will breakdown.

For $m=2$, all degrees of association will be the same. The value close to 1 for m will provide similar behavior as for K-means. For greater value for m, more and more overlapping of clusters will occur.

Running Fuzzy K-means on Mahout

Fuzzy K-means clustering on Mahout runs on Hadoop's MapReduce mode. The algorithm is implemented using MapReduce steps. The implementation is the same as it was for K-means in Mahout. Fuzzy K-means also uses the same vector format as K-means. For the initial set of clusters, you can provide the number of cluster, or Canopy clustering can be used for this. The steps for the MapReduce implementation as given at `https://mahout.apache.org/users/clustering/fuzzy-k-means.html` and are as follows:

1. **Mapper part** reads the input cluster and then computes the cluster membership probability of a point to each cluster. The output key is encoded as `clusterId`. Output values are `ClusterObservations`, which contain the observation statistics.

2. **Combiner part** receives all key-value pairs from the mapper and produces partial sums of the cluster membership probability times input vectors for each cluster. The output key is the encoded cluster identifier. Output values are `ClusterObservations`, which contain observation statistics.

3. In the **Reducers part** multiple reducers receive certain keys and all values associated with those keys. The reducer sums the values to produce a new centroid for the cluster, which is output. The output key is an encoded cluster identifier (for example, "C14"). The output value is a formatted cluster identifier (for example, "C14"). The reducer encodes unconverged clusters with a 'Cn' cluster ID and converged clusters with 'Vn' clusterId.

4. Iteration happens in the driver method, and an iterator iterates over input points and cluster points for a specified number of iterations or until it is converged.

There is a difference in the classes available in the Mahout 0.9 release, which we have here. We do not have `FuzzyKMeansMapper`, `FuzzyKMeansCombiner`, and `FuzzyKMeansReducer` after the 0.6 release, but adjustments are made for this in the `org.apache.mahout.clustering.iterator` package.

Dataset

We will use the liver disorders dataset. This dataset is from BUPA Medical Research Ltd. This database is donated by Richard S. Forsyth. It has seven attributes. More information on this dataset can be found at `https://archive.ics.uci.edu/ml/datasets/Liver+Disorders`.

You can download this dataset from `https://archive.ics.uci.edu/ml/machine-learning-databases/liver-disorders/bupa.data`.

```
← → C  🔒 https://archive.ics.uci.edu/ml/machine-learning-databases/liver-disorders/bupa.data
85,92,45,27,31,0.0,1
85,64,59,32,23,0.0,2
86,54,33,16,54,0.0,2
91,78,34,24,36,0.0,2
87,70,12,28,10,0.0,2
98,55,13,17,17,0.0,2
88,62,20,17,9,0.5,1
88,67,21,11,11,0.5,1
92,54,22,20,7,0.5,1
90,60,25,19,5,0.5,1
89,52,13,24,15,0.5,1
82,62,17,17,15,0.5,1
90,64,61,32,13,0.5,1
86,77,25,19,18,0.5,1
96,67,29,20,11,0.5,1
91,78,20,31,18,0.5,1
89,67,23,16,10,0.5,1
89,79,17,17,16,0.5,1
91,107,20,20,56,0.5,1
94,116,11,33,11,0.5,1
92,59,35,13,19,0.5,1
93,23,35,20,20,0.5,1
90,60,23,27,5,0.5,1
96,68,18,19,19,0.5,1
84,80,47,33,97,0.5,1
92,70,24,13,26,0.5,1
90,47,28,15,18,0.5,1
88,66,20,21,10,0.5,1
91,102,17,13,19,0.5,1
87,41,31,19,16,0.5,1
86,79,28,16,17,0.5,1
91,57,31,23,42,0.5,1
93,77,32,18,29,0.5,1
88,96,28,21,40,0.5,1
94,65,22,18,11,0.5,1
91,72,155,68,82,0.5,2
85,54,47,33,22,0.5,2
79,39,14,19,9,0.5,2
85,85,25,26,30,0.5,2
```

Creating a vector for the dataset

As this is a CSV dataset, we will first have to convert this into the vector format. The following is the code for this:

```
public  void returnVector() throws Exception{
//output path location in HDFS
   Path vecoutput = new Path("<Output path>");
   FileSystem fs = FileSystem.get(getConfiguration());
   //input location of the file in local file system
   Reader r = new FileReader(new File("<Input path location>"));
   SequenceFile.Writer writer;
   //pass the reader to csvvectoriterator
   CSVVectorIterator ctr = new CSVVectorIterator(r);
   writer = new SequenceFile.Writer(fs, getConfiguration(),
      vecoutput, Text.class, VectorWritable.class);
   VectorWritable vec = new VectorWritable();

   while(ctr.hasNext()){
   //write the vector to sequence writer and use key as "Dummy"
   NamedVector nmv = new NamedVector(ctr.next(),"Dummy");
   vec.set(nmv);
   writer.append(new Text( nmv.getName()), vec);

   }
writer.close();
}

//support method to get configuration
private  Configuration getConfiguration(){
   Configuration conf = new Configuration();
   conf.addResource(new Path("/etc/hadoop/conf/core-site.xml"));
   conf.addResource(new Path("/etc/hadoop/conf/hdfs-site.xml"));
   conf.addResource(new Path("/etc/hadoop/conf/yarn-site.xml"));
   return conf;
}
```

Now, your vector is ready. You can also use the vector reader program to inspect this vector.

Vector reader

Let's take a look at the following code:

```
public void readFiles() throws Exception{
  FileSystem fs = null;
  fs = FileSystem.get(getConfiguration());
  //sequence file reader
  SequenceFile.Reader reader = new SequenceFile.Reader(fs,new
    Path("<Vector location>"), getConfiguration());
  Text key = new Text();
  VectorWritable value = new VectorWritable();
  while (reader.next(key, value)) {
    System.out.println(key.toString() + " "+
      value.get().asFormatString());
  }
  reader.close();
}
```

```
Dummy Dummy:{0:85.0,1:92.0,2:45.0,3:27.0,4:31.0,6:1.0}
Dummy Dummy:{0:85.0,1:64.0,2:59.0,3:32.0,4:23.0,6:2.0}
Dummy Dummy:{0:86.0,1:54.0,2:33.0,3:16.0,4:54.0,6:2.0}
Dummy Dummy:{0:91.0,1:78.0,2:34.0,3:24.0,4:36.0,6:2.0}
Dummy Dummy:{0:87.0,1:70.0,2:12.0,3:28.0,4:10.0,6:2.0}
Dummy Dummy:{0:98.0,1:55.0,2:13.0,3:17.0,4:17.0,6:2.0}
Dummy Dummy:{0:88.0,1:62.0,2:20.0,3:17.0,4:9.0,5:0.5,6:1.0}
Dummy Dummy:{0:88.0,1:67.0,2:21.0,3:11.0,4:11.0,5:0.5,6:1.0}
Dummy Dummy:{0:92.0,1:54.0,2:22.0,3:20.0,4:7.0,5:0.5,6:1.0}
Dummy Dummy:{0:90.0,1:60.0,2:25.0,3:19.0,4:5.0,5:0.5,6:1.0}
Dummy Dummy:{0:89.0,1:52.0,2:13.0,3:24.0,4:15.0,5:0.5,6:1.0}
Dummy Dummy:{0:32.0,1:62.0,2:17.0,3:17.0,4:15.0,5:0.5,6:1.0}
Dummy Dummy:{0:90.0,1:64.0,2:61.0,3:32.0,4:13.0,5:0.5,6:1.0}
Dummy Dummy:{0:86.0,1:77.0,2:25.0,3:19.0,4:18.0,5:0.5,6:1.0}
Dummy Dummy:{0:96.0,1:67.0,2:29.0,3:20.0,4:11.0,5:0.5,6:1.0}
Dummy Dummy:{0:91.0,1:78.0,2:20.0,3:31.0,4:18.0,5:0.5,6:1.0}
Dummy Dummy:{0:89.0,1:67.0,2:23.0,3:16.0,4:10.0,5:0.5,6:1.0}
Dummy Dummy:{0:89.0,1:79.0,2:17.0,3:17.0,4:16.0,5:0.5,6:1.0}
Dummy Dummy:{0:91.0,1:107.0,2:20.0,3:20.0,4:56.0,5:0.5,6:1.0}
Dummy Dummy:{0:94.0,1:116.0,2:11.0,3:33.0,4:11.0,5:0.5,6:1.0}
Dummy Dummy:{0:92.0,1:59.0,2:35.0,3:13.0,4:19.0,5:0.5,6:1.0}
Dummy Dummy:{0:93.0,1:23.0,2:35.0,3:20.0,4:20.0,5:0.5,6:1.0}
Dummy Dummy:{0:90.0,1:60.0,2:23.0,3:27.0,4:5.0,5:0.5,6:1.0}
Dummy Dummy:{0:96.0,1:68.0,2:18.0,3:19.0,4:19.0,5:0.5,6:1.0}
Dummy Dummy:{0:84.0,1:80.0,2:47.0,3:33.0,4:97.0,5:0.5,6:1.0}
Dummy Dummy:{0:92.0,1:70.0,2:24.0,3:13.0,4:26.0,5:0.5,6:1.0}
Dummy Dummy:{0:90.0,1:47.0,2:28.0,3:15.0,4:18.0,5:0.5,6:1.0}
Dummy Dummy:{0:88.0,1:66.0,2:20.0,3:21.0,4:10.0,5:0.5,6:1.0}
Dummy Dummy:{0:91.0,1:102.0,2:17.0,3:13.0,4:19.0,5:0.5,6:1.0}
Dummy Dummy:{0:87.0,1:41.0,2:31.0,3:19.0,4:16.0,5:0.5,6:1.0}
```

Now, we will execute the command to run the Fuzzy K-means cluster:

```
bin/mahout  fkmeans -i /user/hue/LDVector/ldvector -c
/user/hue/fkcluster -o /user/hue/kfuzzycentriods -cd 1.0 -k 4 -m
1.01 -x 5 -dm
org.apache.mahout.common.distance.EuclideanDistanceMeasure
-cl -xm mapreduce
```

- -i: This is the input vector that has a directory
- -o: This is the output file path containing the clusters
- -c: This is the initial cluster path (empty file, in this case)
- -dm: This is the distance measure used in the algorithm
- -cd: This is the convergence delta
- -k: This is the number of clusters
- -m: This is the fuzziness factor
- -x: This is the maximum number of iterations
- -cl: This is the a Boolean indicating that if `true`, that the clustering step is to be executed after clusters have been determined
- -xm: This is the execution method sequential or MapReduce

Run the cluster dumper utility to dump the output to the text file:

```
bin/mahout  clusterdump -i /user/hue/kfuzzycentriods/clusters-5-
final -o  /user/hue/clusterdumpKfuzzy.txt -dt sequencefile --
pointsDir /user/hue/kfuzzycentriods/clusteredPoints
```

Now, open your file and you can see the clusters created. It informs you about the number of points in the cluster 'n', center of the cluster 'c', radius of the cluster 'r', and all the points in the cluster.

Visualizing clusters

Mahout under the Mahout-example package provides the classes to generate a sample dataset. In this class, it runs the reference clustering implementations over them.

For Fuzzy K-means, `DisplayFuzzyKmeans` is the class that displays the cluster. You can directly run the class. As per the code in the class, points are generated as follows:

```
generateSamples(500, 1, 1, 3); // 500  samples of sd 3
generateSamples(300, 1, 0, 0.5); //300 sample of sd 0.5
generateSamples(300, 0, 2, 0.1); //300 sample of sd 0.1
```

Once you will run this class, you will view the clusters, as shown here:

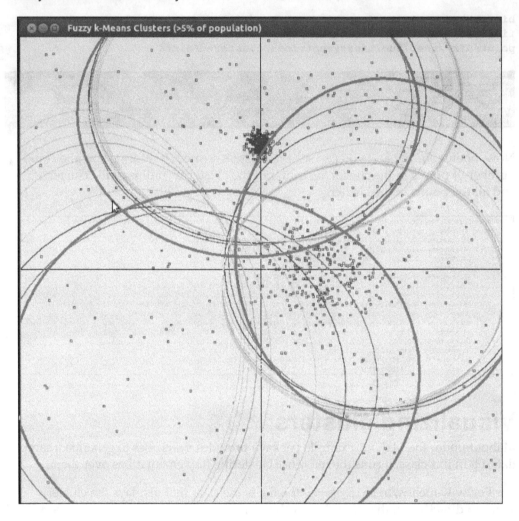

The bold red color is the final clustering done by the algorithm. In the console, you can find the output related to the generation of points and cluster formation.

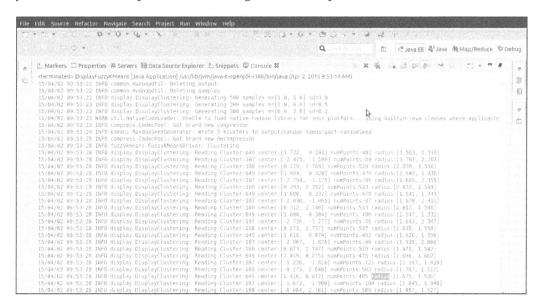

Summary

We discussed Fuzzy K-means clustering in this chapter. We saw how fuzzy the K-means clustering algorithm works and is used in the Mahout implementation of the Fuzzy K-means algorithm on the liver disorder dataset. We discussed how Fuzzy K-means is implemented using the map reduce method. We implemented the code to convert the CSV file into a Mahout useable vector format. We used a vector reader program to read the generated vector. We used a cluster dumper utility to view the output of the cluster.

Now, we will move on to the next chapter where we will discuss the model-based clustering algorithm.

5
Understanding Model-based Clustering

In the previous chapters, we discussed K-means, Fuzzy K-means, and Canopy clustering. In this chapter, we will discuss the model-based clustering algorithm. Model-based clustering is used to overcome some of the deficiencies that can occur in the K-means or Fuzzy K-means algorithms. We will discuss the following topics in this chapter:

- Learning model-based clustering
- Understanding Dirichlet clustering
- Understanding topic modeling

Learning model-based clustering

In model-based clustering, we assume that data is generated by a model and tries to get the model from the data. The right model will fit the data better than other models.

In the K-means algorithm, we provide the initial set of clusters and K-means provides us with the data points in the clusters. Think about a case where clusters are not distributed normally, then the improvement of the cluster will not be effective using k-means. In this scenario, the model-based clustering algorithm will do the job. You can think of another method when dividing the clusters, that is, hierarchical clustering in which we will need to find the overlapping information. This situation will also be covered by model-based clustering algorithms.

If all the components are not well separated, a cluster can consist of multiple mixture components. In simple terms, in model-based clustering, data is a mixture of two or more components. Each component has an associated probability and each component is described by a density function. Model-based clustering can capture hierarchy and overlap the clusters at the same time. Partitions are determined by an **expectation-maximization** (**EM**) algorithm for maximum likelihood. Generated models are compared using the **Bayesian information criterion** (**BIC**). The model with the lowest BIC is preferred:

$$BIC = -2 \, log(L) + mlog(n)$$

Here, L is the likelihood function, m is the number of free parameters to be estimated, and n is the number of data points.

Understanding Dirichlet clustering

Dirichlet clustering is the model-based clustering method. This algorithm is used to understand the data and cluster the data. Dirichlet clustering is a process of nonparametric and Bayesian modeling. It is nonparametric because it can have an infinite number of parameters. Dirichlet clustering is based on the Dirichlet distribution.

For this algorithm, we have a probabilistic mixture of a number of models that are used to explain data. Each data point will emerge from one of the available models. Models are taken from the sample of prior distribution of models and points are assigning to those models iteratively. In each iteration probability, a point is generated by a particular model is calculated. After points are assigned to models, new parameters for each model are sampled. This sample is from the posterior distribution for the model parameters and it considers all of the observed data points assigned to the model. This sampling provides more information than normal clustering which is clear from these two points:

- Because we are assigning points to different models, we can find out how many models are supported by data
- We can get other information such as how well data is described by the model and how two points are explained by the same model

Topic modeling

In machine learning, topic modeling is nothing but finding a topic from the text document using a statistical model. A document on particular topics has some particular words. For example, if you are reading an article on sports, there is a high chance that you will get words like football, baseball, formula one, Olympics, and so on. So, a topic model actually uncovers the hidden sense of the article or document. Topic models are nothing but algorithms that can discover the main themes from the large set of unstructured documents. Topic modeling uncovers the semantic structure of the text and enables us to organize large scale electronic archives. Mahout has the implementation of one of the topic modeling algorithms—**Latent Dirichlet allocation (LDA)**.

LDA is a statistical model of document collection that tries to capture the intuition of the documents. In normal clustering algorithms, if words having the same meaning don't occur together, then the algorithm will not associate them, but LDA can find out which two words are used in a similar context and find out the association. In this way, LDA is better than other algorithms.

LDA is a *generative probabilistic* model. It is generative because the model is tweaked to fit the data, and using the parameters of the model, we can generate the data on which it fits. It is probabilistic because each topic is modeled as an infinite mixture over an underlying set of topic probabilities. The topic probabilities provide an explicit representation of a document. Graphically, an LDA model can be represented as follows:

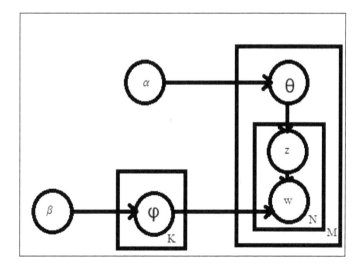

The notations used in this figure are described here:

- **M, N,** and **K** represent the number of documents, the number of words in the document, and the number of topics in the document respectively.
- α is the prior weight of the topic k in the document
- β is the prior weight of the word w in a topic
- φ is the probability of a word occurring in a topic
- Θ is the topic of distribution
- **Z** is the identity of topic of all words in all documents.
- **W** is the identity of all the words in all the documents.

How does LDA work in the MapReduce mode? These are the steps that LDA follows in the mapper and reducer steps:

Mapper phase:

- Program starts with an empty topic model
- All the documents are read by different mappers
- Probabilities are calculated of each topic for each word in the document

Reducer phase:

- Reducer receives the count of probabilities
- These counts are summed and model is normalized

This process is iterative, and in each iteration, the sum of the probabilities is calculated and the process stops when it stops changing. A parameter set that is similar to the convergence threshold in K-means is set to check the changes. In the end, LDA estimates how well the model fits the data.

In Mahout, the Collapsed Variation Bayes algorithm is implemented for LDA. LDA uses the term frequency vector as an input and not as TF-IDF vectors. We need to take care of the two parameters while running the LDA algorithm — the number of topics and the number of words in the documents. A large number of topics will provide a lower level of topics while a lower number will provide a generalized topic at a high level such as sports.

Mapper reads the matrix of the size number of topics into the number of features or words. So, improving the speed depends on the selection of features or words.

In Mahout, to estimate the model's mean field, variational inference is used. It is similar to expectation-maximization of hierarchical Bayesian models. The Expectation step reads each document and calculates the probability of each topic for each word in every document.

The Maximization step takes the counts and summed all probabilities and normalizes them.

Running LDA using Mahout

To run LDA using Mahout, we will use a 20newsgroups dataset. We will convert the corpus into vectors, run LDA on those vectors, and get the resultant topics.

Let's run this example to view how topic modeling works in Mahout.

Dataset selection

We will use 20newsgroups dataset for this exercise. Download the dataset 20news-bydate.tar.gz from http://qwone.com/~jason/20Newsgroups/.

Steps to execute CVB (LDA)

1. Create a directory 20newsdata and unzip the data here:

   ```
   mkdir /tmp/20newsdata
   cdtmp/20newsdata
   tar-xzvf /tmp/20news-bydate.tar.gz
   ```

2. There are two folders under 20newsdata, 20news-bydate-test, and 20news-bydate-train. Now, create another directory 20newsdataall and merge both training and test data of the group.

3. Now, move to the home directory and execute the following command:

   ```
   mkdir /tmp/20newsdataall
   cp -R /20newsdata/*/* /tmp/20newsdataall
   ```

4. Create a directory in Hadoop and save this data in HDFS:

   ```
   hadoopfs -mkdir /usr/hue/20newsdata
   hadoopfs -put /tmp/20newsdataall /usr/hue/20newsdata
   ```

5. Mahout CVB will accept data in the vector format. For this, we will first generate a sequence file from the directory:

```
bin/mahoutseqdirectory -i /user/hue/20newsdata/20newsdataall
-o /user/hue/20newsdataseq-out
```

6. Convert the sequence file into a sparse vector but, as discussed earlier, using term frequency weight:

```
bin/mahout seq2sparse -i /user/hue/20newsdataseq-out/part-m-
00000 -o /user/hue/20newsdatavec -lnorm -nv -wttf
```

```
[root@sandbox ~]# mahout seq2sparse -i /user/hue/20newsdataseq-out/part-m-00000 -o /user/hue/20newsdatavec -lnorm -nv -wt tf
MAHOUT_LOCAL is not set; adding HADOOP_CONF_DIR to classpath.
Running on hadoop, using /usr/lib/hadoop/bin/hadoop and HADOOP_CONF_DIR=/etc/hadoop/conf
MAHOUT-JOB: /usr/lib/mahout/mahout-examples-0.9.0.2.1.1.0-385-job.jar
15/04/19 01:02:57 INFO vectorizer.SparseVectorsFromSequenceFiles: Maximum n-gram size is: 1
15/04/19 01:02:57 INFO vectorizer.SparseVectorsFromSequenceFiles: Minimum LLR value: 1.0
15/04/19 01:02:57 INFO vectorizer.SparseVectorsFromSequenceFiles: Number of reduce tasks: 1
15/04/19 01:02:57 INFO vectorizer.SparseVectorsFromSequenceFiles: Tokenizing documents in /user/hue/20newsdataseq-out/part-m-00000
15/04/19 01:03:02 INFO client.RMProxy: Connecting to ResourceManager at sandbox.hortonworks.com/10.0.2.15:8050
15/04/19 01:03:10 INFO input.FileInputFormat: Total input paths to process : 1
15/04/19 01:03:11 INFO mapreduce.JobSubmitter: number of splits:1
15/04/19 01:03:12 INFO mapreduce.JobSubmitter: Submitting tokens for job: job_1429428374925_0001
15/04/19 01:03:13 INFO impl.YarnClientImpl: Submitted application application_1429428374925_0001
15/04/19 01:03:14 INFO mapreduce.Job: The url to track the job: http://sandbox.hortonworks.com:8088/proxy/application_1429428374925_0001/
15/04/19 01:03:14 INFO mapreduce.Job: Running job: job_1429428374925_0001
15/04/19 01:04:07 INFO mapreduce.Job: Job job_1429428374925_0001 running in uber mode : false
15/04/19 01:04:07 INFO mapreduce.Job:  map 0% reduce 0%
15/04/19 01:04:36 INFO mapreduce.Job:  map 67% reduce 0%
15/04/19 01:04:39 INFO mapreduce.Job:  map 100% reduce 0%
15/04/19 01:04:46 INFO mapreduce.Job: Job job_1429428374925_0001 completed successfully
15/04/19 01:04:48 INFO mapreduce.Job: Counters: 30
       File System Counters
```

7. Convert the sparse vector to the input form required by the CVB algorithm:

```
bin/mahoutrowid -i /user/hue/20newsdatavec/tf-vectors   -o
/user/hue/20newsmatrix
```

```
[root@sandbox ~]# mahout rowid -i /user/hue/20newsdatavec/tf-vectors -o /user/hue/20newsmatrix
MAHOUT_LOCAL is not set; adding HADOOP_CONF_DIR to classpath.
Running on hadoop, using /usr/lib/hadoop/bin/hadoop and HADOOP_CONF_DIR=/etc/hadoop/conf
MAHOUT-JOB: /usr/lib/mahout/mahout-examples-0.9.0.2.1.1.0-385-job.jar
15/04/19 01:34:25 INFO common.AbstractJob: Command line arguments: {--endPhase=[2147483647], --input=[/user/hue/20newsdatavec/tf-vectors], --output=[/user/hue/20newsmatrix], --startPhase=[0], --tempDir=[temp]}
15/04/19 01:34:29 INFO zlib.ZlibFactory: Successfully loaded & initialized native-zlib library
15/04/19 01:34:29 INFO compress.CodecPool: Got brand-new compressor [.deflate]
15/04/19 01:34:29 INFO compress.CodecPool: Got brand-new compressor [.deflate]
15/04/19 01:34:35 INFO vectors.RowIdJob: Wrote out matrix with 18846 rows and 93563 columns to /user/hue/20newsmatrix/matrix
15/04/19 01:34:36 INFO driver.MahoutDriver: Program took 12828 ms (Minutes: 0.2138)
```

8. Convert the sparse vector to the input form required by the CVB algorithm:

```
bin/mahout cvb -i /user/hue/20newsmatrix/matrix -o
/user/hue/ldaoutput-k 10 -x 20 -
dict/user/hue/20newsdatavec/dictionary.file-0 -dt
/user/hue/ldatopics -mt /user/hue/ldamodel
```

   ○ -i: This is the input path of the document vector

   ○ -o: This is the output path of topic term distribution

   ○ -k: This is the number of latent topics

   ○ -x: This is the max number of iteration

   ○ -dict: This is the term dictionary files

°   -dt: This is the output path of document-topic distribution

°   -mt: This is the model state path after each iteration

```
[root@sandbox ~]# mahout cvb -i /user/hue/20newsmatrix/matrix -o /user/hue/ldaoutput -x 20 -k 10 -dict /user/hue/20newsdatavec/dictionary.file-0 -dt /user/hue/ldatopic
-mt /user/hue/ldamodel
MAHOUT LOCAL is not set; adding HADOOP_CONF_DIR to classpath.
Running on hadoop, using /usr/lib/hadoop/bin/hadoop and HADOOP_CONF_DIR=/etc/hadoop/conf
MAHOUT-JOB: /usr/lib/mahout/mahout-examples-0.9.0.2.1.1.0-385-job.jar
15/04/19 02:10:47 WARN driver.MahoutDriver: No cvb.props found on classpath, will use command-line arguments only
15/04/19 02:10:49 INFO common.AbstractJob: Command line arguments: {--convergenceDelta=[0.0], --dictionary=[/user/hue/20newsdatavec/dictionary.file-0], --doc_topic_outp
ut=[/user/hue/ldatopic], --doc_topic_smoothing=[1.0E-4], --endPhase=[2147483647], --input=[/user/hue/20newsmatrix/matrix], --iteration_block_size=[10], --maxIter=[20],
--max_doc_topic_iters=[10], --num_reduce_tasks=[10], --num_train_threads=[4], --num_topics=[10], --num_update_threads=[1], --output=[/user/hue/ldaoutput], --startPhase=
[0], --tempDir=[temp], --term_topic_smoothing=[1.0E-4], --test_set_fraction=[0.0], --topic_model_temp_dir=[/user/hue/ldamodel]}
15/04/19 02:10:57 INFO cvb.CVB0Driver: Will run Collapsed Variational Bayes (0th-derivative approximation) learning for LDA on /user/hue/20newsmatrix/matrix (numTerms:
93563), finding 10-topics, with document/topic prior 1.0E-4, topic/term prior 1.0E-4. Maximum iterations to run will be 20, unless the change in perplexity is less tha
n 0.0.  Topic model output (p(term|topic) for each topic) will be stored /user/hue/ldaoutput.  Random initialization seed is 8319, holding out 0.0 of the data for perpl
exity check

15/04/19 02:10:57 INFO cvb.CVB0Driver: Dictionary to be used located /user/hue/20newsdatavec/dictionary.file-0
p(topic|docId) will be stored /user/hue/ldatopic

15/04/19 02:10:57 INFO cvb.CVB0Driver: Current iteration number: 0
15/04/19 02:10:57 INFO cvb.CVB0Driver: About to run iteration 1 of 20
15/04/19 02:10:57 INFO cvb.CVB0Driver: About to run: Iteration 1 of 20, input path: /user/hue/ldamodel/model-0
15/04/19 02:10:57 INFO Configuration.deprecation: mapred.input.dir is deprecated. Instead, use mapreduce.input.fileinputformat.inputdir
15/04/19 02:10:57 INFO Configuration.deprecation: mapred.compress.map.output is deprecated. Instead, use mapreduce.map.output.compress
15/04/19 02:10:57 INFO Configuration.deprecation: mapred.output.dir is deprecated. Instead, use mapreduce.output.fileoutputformat.outputdir
15/04/19 02:10:57 INFO client.RMProxy: Connecting to ResourceManager at sandbox.hortonworks.com/10.0.2.15:8050
15/04/19 02:11:04 INFO input.FileInputFormat: Total input paths to process : 1
15/04/19 02:11:06 INFO mapreduce.JobSubmitter: number of splits:1
15/04/19 02:11:07 INFO mapreduce.JobSubmitter: Submitting tokens for job: job_1429428374925_0008
15/04/19 02:11:09 INFO impl.YarnClientImpl: Submitted application application_1429428374925_0008
15/04/19 02:11:10 INFO mapreduce.Job: The url to track the job: http://sandbox.hortonworks.com:8088/proxy/application_1429428374925_0008/
15/04/19 02:11:10 INFO mapreduce.Job: Running job: job_1429428374925_0008
15/04/19 02:11:49 INFO mapreduce.Job: Job job_1429428374925_0008 running in uber mode : false
15/04/19 02:11:49 INFO mapreduce.Job:  map 0% reduce 0%
```

9.   Once the command has been executed, you will get the following info on the screen:

```
15/04/20 11:37:18 INFO cvb.CVB0Driver: Completed 10 iterations in 4236 seconds
15/04/20 11:37:18 INFO cvb.CVB0Driver: Perplexities: ()
15/04/20 11:37:18 INFO cvb.CVB0Driver: About to run: Writing final topic/term distributions from /user/hue/ldamodel/model-10 to /user/hue/ldaoutput
15/04/20 11:37:32 INFO client.RMProxy: Connecting to ResourceManager at sandbox.hortonworks.com/10.0.2.15:8050
15/04/20 11:38:06 INFO input.FileInputFormat: Total input paths to process : 10
15/04/20 11:38:15 INFO mapreduce.JobSubmitter: number of splits:10
15/04/20 11:38:18 INFO mapreduce.JobSubmitter: Submitting tokens for job: job_1429543935099_0019
15/04/20 11:38:23 INFO impl.YarnClientImpl: Submitted application application_1429543935099_0019
15/04/20 11:38:23 INFO mapreduce.Job: The url to track the job: http://sandbox.hortonworks.com:8088/proxy/application_1429543935099_0019/
15/04/20 11:38:23 INFO cvb.CVB0Driver: About to run: Writing final document/topic inference from /user/hue/20newsmatrix/matrix to /user/hue/ldatopic
```

10.   To view the output, run the following command:

```
bin/mahout vectordump -i /user/hue/ldaoutput/ -d
/user/hue/20newsdatavec/dictionary.file-0 -dtsequencefile -vs
10 -sort true -o /tmp/lda-output.txt
```

°   -i: This is the input location of the cvb output

°   -d: This is the dictionary file location created during vector creation

°   -dt: This is the dictionary file type (sequence or text)

°   -vs: This is the vector size

°   -sort flag: This is the to put true or false

°   -o: This is the output location of the local filesystem

```
[root@sandbox ~]# mahout vectordump -i /user/hue/ldaoutput/ -d /user/hue/20newsdatavec/dictionary.file-0 -dt sequencefile -vs 10 -sort true -o /user/hue/lda-output.txt
MAHOUT LOCAL is not set; adding HADOOP_CONF_DIR to classpath.
Running on hadoop, using /usr/lib/hadoop/bin/hadoop and HADOOP_CONF_DIR=/etc/hadoop/conf
MAHOUT-JOB: /usr/lib/mahout/mahout-examples-0.9.0.2.1.1.0-385-job.jar
15/04/21 01:26:29 INFO common.AbstractJob: Command line arguments: { --dictionary=[/user/hue/20newsdatavec/dictionary.file-0], --dictionaryType=[sequencefile], --endPhas
e=[2147483647], --input=[/user/hue/ldaoutput/], --output=[/user/hue/lda-output.txt], --sortVectors=[true], --startPhase=[0], --tempDir=[temp], --vectorSize=[10]}
15/04/21 01:26:48 INFO vectors.VectorDumper: Sort? true
15/04/21 01:26:50 INFO vectors.VectorDumper: Output file: /user/hue/lda-output.txt
```

11. Now, your output will be saved in the local filesystem. Open the file and you will see an output similar to the following:

```
space:0.022345160159105454,
nasa:0.006661446955357236,
shuttle:0.005303426588958789,
software:0.004067928814028095,
organization:0.004029704892213813,
launch:0.005962498876058316,
earth:0.0049667585661688895,
mission:0.005323293651301655,
```

As you can see in the preceding screenshot, after running the algorithm, you will get the term and probability of that term.

Summary

In this chapter, you learned about model-based clustering, the Dirichlet process, and topic modeling. In model-based clustering, we try to get model from the data, while the Dirichlet process is used to understand the data. Topic modeling helps us to identify the topics in an article or in a set of documents. We discussed how Mahout has implemented topic modeling using the latent Dirichlet process and how it is implemented in map reduce.

We also discussed how to use Mahout to find the topic of distribution on the set of documents. In the next chapter, we will discuss one more new algorithm—Streaming K-means.

6
Understanding Streaming K-means

In the previous chapters, we discussed model-based clustering algorithms. In this chapter, we will discuss one more new algorithm that is implemented in Apache Mahout – Streaming K-means. The algorithms, which we used to build models, generally find patterns in the data and use this learned pattern to predict from the incoming data. In this scenario, we know that patterns in data are static, but the main difficulty occurs when the patterns in data are dynamic. In the scenario where patterns in data are dynamic, streaming algorithms comes to the rescue. We will discuss the following topics in this chapter:

- Learning Streaming K-means
- Using Mahout to run Streaming K-means

Learning Streaming K-means

Streaming K-means algorithms are applied when data comes in a stream and we want to estimate the clusters dynamically. Streaming the K-means algorithm is based on the paper *Fast and Accurate K-Means for Large Datasets* by M. Schindler, A. Wong, and A. Meyerson.

This paper can be found at `http://papers.nips.cc/paper/4362-fast-and-accurate-k-means-for-large-datasets.pdf`.

The algorithm uses the *O (k logn)* memory, runs in the *O (nk log n)* time, and obtains an *O (1)* worst-case approximation. The streaming step passes the clusters to the BallKMeans step. This step moves the points to the center of the mass of the samples and further reduces the number of clusters down to K.

In Mahout, Streaming K-means is implemented using two steps:

- Streaming Step
- BallKMeans

As Ted Dunning (who has contributed to Mahout clustering, classification, and matrix decomposition algorithms, and has helped expand the new version of Mahout Math library) recently mentioned (in a Mahout user group e-mail), in Mahout, the idea is that we want to do single pass high quality clustering of a lot of data. This is hard to do with traditional K-means, both because K-means normally requires multiple passes through the data to get good centroids and also because multiple restarts are required to get good results. A streaming solution should also be able to give you an accurate clustering at any point in time with roughly *unit-ish* cost.

Let's discuss the Streaming step and BallKMeans step in more detail.

The Streaming step

The Streaming step can be understood as a dimensionality reduction step. Mahout's implementation of the Streaming step is different. It does not take data stream size into consideration. The algorithm works in this way:

- It takes the first point from the data stream and makes it the centroid of the cluster.
- It takes the second point and measures the distance from the first point. If the distance is greater than the distance parameter `distanceCutoff`, it creates a new cluster with a new point as the centroid; otherwise, it joins the point into an existing cluster and recalculates the centroid.

So, after processing a new point, there will be as many clusters as there were before the new point, or there will be one more addition to the number of clusters. The process can be understood by the following points and figures:

- Consider a new point from the dataset
- This point will become a centroid
- Now, when the second point arrives, its distance from the first point is calculated

- If the distance calculated is more than the distance cut off, the second point will also be converted as a centroid for the next cluster:

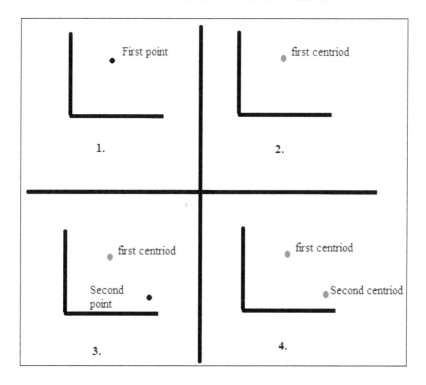

- On arrival of the third point, distance is again calculated, and if it is found to be near the first centroid, it becomes a part of the first cluster and the centroid is recalculated.

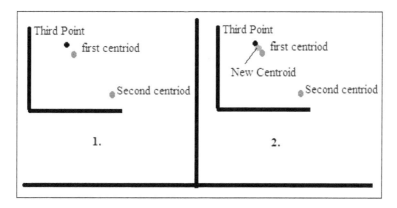

The pseudo code for Streaming K-means is as follows:

- For each point p with weight w, find the closest centroid to p, call this centroid c, and call the distance between p and c as d

- If there is an event with probability $d*w/distanceCutoff$ occurs, create a new cluster with p as the centroid, or else merge p and c

- If there are too many clusters, increase the distance CutOff and cluster recursively

As the number of clusters increases, the algorithm will use the following formula to limit the number of clusters:

*clusterOvershoot * numClusters*

clusterOvershoot has a default value of 2. It is a multiplicative slack factor.

The algorithm shoots for an optimal number of clusters and this number is numclusters. With more data at runtime, this number can increase.

As the number of clusters grows, formed clusters are reclustered to a smaller number. If the number is still high, distanceCutoff is increased. At runtime, based on the size of the data stream, the algorithm evaluates the parameters. The following are the parameters that this algorithm takes as input:

- distanceCutOff: As discussed in the earlier paragraph, distanceCutOff is used to check whether a new point will be the new centroid or a point in an existing cluster. (*1.0/numofClusters*) is the default value. distanceCutOff grows as geometric progression and beta, explained ahead, works as a common ratio.

- Beta: Growth of the distanceCutOff parameter is controlled by beta. As distanceCutOff increases as a geometric progression, beta works as a common ratio. The default value for beta is 1.3.

- clusterOvershoot: This is multiplicative stack factor that slows down the collapsing of clusters. The default value is 2.

- clusterLogFactor: This is used to estimate the number of clusters to be produced by the Streaming step at runtime. The formula used is as follows:

*clusterLogFactor*Math.log(numProcessedDataPoints)*

- numClusters: This number is the algorithm guess for the number of clusters it is shooting for. This number should not be set to the final number that we are expecting as an output of the algorithm.

- Related information on this topic can be found at `https://mahout.apache.org/users/clustering/streaming-k-means.html`.

Now, move to the second step of the streaming algorithm, that is, the **BallKMeans** step.

The BallKMeans step

The **BallKMeans** algorithm takes weighted vectors with probabilistic seeding. This is similar to K-means++. This algorithm also has two stages:

- Seeding
- BallKMeans

The reference for this class of algorithms is defined in *The Effectiveness of Lloyd-Type methods for the k-Means Problem* by Rafail Ostrovsky, Yuval Rabani, Leonard J. Schulman, and Chaitanya Swamy. The BallKMeans step is implemented as described in section 4.2 of this paper, and the seeding step is as defined under section 4.1.1 of this paper.

The seeding stage of this algorithm is an initial estimation where the centroid should be, and this estimate is improved using the BallKMeans step.

This algorithm can be run with multiple independent runs and it will select the best solution from all executions. In each run, the seeding step is used to select K-centroids, and BallKMeans is run iteratively to refine the solution. The seeding step can be set in two ways, either by KMeans++, or uniformly at random. The recommended way is to use KMeans++ because it provides better results. There is a Boolean parameter to set for this option, which if `true`, that takes the seeding method as KMeans++.

The incoming data can be converted into a test and training dataset, which depends on one of the parameters, `testProbability`. If this parameter is 0 or the `numRuns` parameter is 1, then the entire dataset is used for both training and testing; if it has a value between 0 and 1, data is partitioned into two groups — a testing dataset of size value*the total size of data and training dataset of size (1-value)* total size of data. After the seeding and BallKMeans steps are run on the training dataset, the cost is calculated using the test dataset. In each iteration of BallKMeans, clusters are formed by assigning each data point to the nearest centroid and the center of mass of the trimmed cluster becomes the new centroid. The following are the parameters that are used by this algorithm:

- `numRuns`: This indicates the number of iterations to be performed. The default run is 1.

- `testProbabilty`: As discussed, this parameter indicates whether there will be a split in the dataset or not. If the value is between 0 and 1, the dataset will be split into a testdata of size testprobability*size of dataset and training data of size (1-testprobabilty)*size of dataset.

- `correctWeigths`: This is a Boolean variable and if it is `true`, outliers are considered for calculating the weight of the centroids. However, outliers will not be considered while calculating the position of the cluster. The default value is `true`.

- `numClusters`: This is the number of centroids to be returned. This number of centroids will be returned by the algorithms.

- `trimFraction`: Let's say that we have a point `p` and the nearest centroid is `c`. If the distance from `p` to `c` is greater than trimFraction * d, then `p` is considered an outlier during that iteration of `BallKMeans` and will be ignored. The default value is 9/10.

- `maxNumIterations`: This parameter will decide after the seeding step how many times the iterative clustering process will run. Increasing this number will increase the accuracy of the result but at the expense of runtime. The recommended value is 1 or 2.

- `kMeansPlusPlusInit`: This parameter is a Boolean variable and decides of the seeding method. If it is `true`, the K-means++ method will be selected; otherwise, it will be uniform at random. The default value is `true`.

Now we are clear about the steps, let's move and find out how we can use the Mahout implementation to stream the K-means algorithm.

Using Mahout for streaming K-means

After understanding the algorithm side, let's see how we can use the Mahout implementation of Streaming K-means.

Dataset selection

To run the Streaming K-means, we will first select a dataset. The reference paper *Fast and Accurate K-Means for Large Datasets*, by M.Schindler, A.Wong, and A.Meyerson mentioned two datasets that they used — **BigCross** and **Census1990**.

Here, we will use the Census1990 dataset. This dataset can be downloaded from `https://archive.ics.uci.edu/ml/machine-learning-databases/census1990-mld/`.

This dataset has 2458285 number of instances and 68 number of attributes. Once you have download this data, you will notice that it is in the CSV format, and we cannot use this directly in Mahout.

Converting CSV to a vector file

You can use the following mentioned code to convert your CSV file to a Mahout readable vector.

This code is almost the same as that mentioned in *Chapter 2, Understanding K-means Clustering*:

```
public String getSeqFile(String inputLocation) throws Exception{
  double[]colvalues = new double[68];
  String outputPath= <output location at hdfs>;
  Path vecoutput =new Path(outputPath);
  FileSystemfs = null;
  SequenceFile.Writer writer;
  fs = FileSystem.get(getConfiguration());
  checkAndCreatePath(inputLocation);
  writer = new SequenceFile.Writer
    (fs, getConfiguration(),vecoutput, Text.class,
    VectorWritable.class);
  VectorWritablevec = new VectorWritable();
  try {
    FileReaderfr = new FileReader(inputLocation);
    BufferedReaderbr = new BufferedReader(fr);
    String s = null;
    String key="";
    while((s=br.readLine())!=null){
      String spl[] = s.split(getFileSperator());
      Integer val = 0;
      for(int i=1;i<spl.length;i++){
        key = spl[0].toString();
        colvalues[val++] = Double.parseDouble(spl[i]);
        }
      NamedVectornmv = new NamedVector
        (new DenseVector(colvalues),key);
      vec.set(nmv);
      writer.append(new Text(nmv.getName()), vec);
      }
    writer.close();
  } catch (Exception e) {
```

```
    System.out.println("ERROR: "+e);
  }
  return outputPath;
}
```

Pass your input downloaded file to this method, and this will provide the vector created at the location given by you.

You can read this vector using the Vector Reader program as provided in *Chapter 4, Understanding the Fuzzy K-means Algorithm Using Mahout*. You will see an output similar to the following screenshot:

Running Streaming K-means

Now that we have our vector ready, use the following command to execute the following algorithm:

```
bin/mahout streamingkmeans -i /user/hue/SKmeansVec -o
/user/hue/SKmeansOut -km 72 -s 2 -k 12 -nbkm 3 -d
morg.apache.mahout.common.distance.EuclideanDistanceMeasure-
scorg.apache.mahout.math.neighborhood.FastProjectionSearch
```

- -i: This is the input path of the vector

- -o: This is the output path

- -km: This is the estimated number of clusters to be used for the Map phase of the job when running StreamingKMeans. It should be around *k*log(n)*, which, in this case, is around 72 (*k*=12 and *n* = 2458285).

- -s: This is the search size. The number of elements whose distances from the query vector is actually computer is proportion to searchSize. If no value is given, it defaults to 1.

- -k: This is the K in K-means, and this will approximately be the number of generated clusters.

- -nbkmnumBallKMeansRuns: This is the number of `BallKMeans` runs to be used at the end, to try to cluster the points. If no value is given, it defaults to 4.

- `-dm`: This is the class name of the distance measure

- `-sc`: This is the searcher class. It is the type of searcher to be used when performing the nearest neighbor searches. This defaults to `ProjectionSearch`.

The full list of parameters can be found by typing the `streamingKmeans` command on the console.

```
15/06/16 07:48:13 INFO mapreduce.StreamingKMeansDriver: Starting StreamingKMeans clustering for vectors in /user/hue/SKmeansVec; results are output to /user/hue/SKmeans
Out
15/06/16 07:48:26 INFO Configuration.deprecation: mapred.input.dir is deprecated. Instead, use mapreduce.input.fileinputformat.inputdir
15/06/16 07:48:26 INFO Configuration.deprecation: mapred.compress.map.output is deprecated. Instead, use mapreduce.map.output.compress
15/06/16 07:48:26 INFO Configuration.deprecation: mapred.output.dir is deprecated. Instead, use mapreduce.output.fileoutputformat.outputdir
15/06/16 07:48:29 INFO client.RMProxy: Connecting to ResourceManager at sandbox.hortonworks.com/10.0.2.15:8050
15/06/16 07:48:48 INFO input.FileInputFormat: Total input paths to process : 1
15/06/16 07:48:48 INFO mapreduce.JobSubmitter: number of splits:1
15/06/16 07:48:50 INFO mapreduce.JobSubmitter: Submitting tokens for job: job_1434464895156_0001
15/06/16 07:48:51 INFO impl.YarnClientImpl: Submitted application application_1434464895156_0001
15/06/16 07:48:51 INFO mapreduce.Job: The url to track the job: http://sandbox.hortonworks.com:8088/proxy/application_1434464895156_0001/
15/06/16 07:48:51 INFO mapreduce.Job: Running job: job_1434464895156_0001
15/06/16 07:50:33 INFO mapreduce.Job: Job job_1434464895156_0001 running in uber mode : false
15/06/16 07:50:33 INFO mapreduce.Job:  map 0% reduce 0%
15/06/16 07:52:34 INFO mapreduce.Job:  map 11% reduce 0%
15/06/16 07:52:37 INFO mapreduce.Job:  map 44% reduce 0%
15/06/16 07:52:39 INFO mapreduce.Job:  map 100% reduce 0%
15/06/16 07:53:05 INFO mapreduce.Job:  map 100% reduce 100%
15/06/16 07:53:07 INFO mapreduce.Job: Job job_1434464895156_0001 completed successfully
15/06/16 07:53:08 INFO mapreduce.Job: Counters: 49
        File System Counters
                FILE: Number of bytes read=73103
                FILE: Number of bytes written=349365
                FILE: Number of read operations=0
                FILE: Number of large read operations=0
                FILE: Number of write operations=0
                HDFS: Number of bytes read=29438752
                HDFS: Number of bytes written=4705
                HDFS: Number of read operations=7
                HDFS: Number of large read operations=0
                HDFS: Number of write operations=2
```

```
        Map-Reduce Framework
                Map input records=51466
                Map output records=308
                Map output bytes=173096
                Map output materialized bytes=73095
                Input split bytes=120
                Combine input records=0
                Combine output records=0
                Reduce input groups=1
                Reduce shuffle bytes=73095
                Reduce input records=308
                Reduce output records=8
                Spilled Records=616
                Shuffled Maps =1
                Failed Shuffles=0
                Merged Map outputs=1
                GC time elapsed (ms)=479
                CPU time spent (ms)=15100
                Physical memory (bytes) snapshot=334274560
                Virtual memory (bytes) snapshot=1825820672
                Total committed heap usage (bytes)=164626432
        Shuffle Errors
                BAD_ID=0
                CONNECTION=0
                IO_ERROR=0
                WRONG_LENGTH=0
                WRONG_MAP=0
                WRONG_REDUCE=0
        File Input Format Counters
                Bytes Read=29438632
        File Output Format Counters
                Bytes Written=4705
15/06/16 07:53:08 INFO mapreduce.StreamingKMeansDriver: StreamingKMeans clustering complete. Results are in /user/hue/SKmeansOut. Took 281753 ms
15/06/16 07:53:08 INFO driver.MahoutDriver: Program took 299121 ms (Minutes: 4.98535)
```

The output will be created in the given output directory and, unlike the K-means output, this will contain only one file. To view this file, use the `seqdumper` command:

```
mahoutseqdumper -i /user/hue/SKmeansOut/part-r-00000 -o
/user/hue/streamingKmeans.txt
```

- `-i`: This is the input that is the output of the previous command
- `-o`: This is the location in local filesystem for output

This output can be seen using the `cat` command on the console. The output will look like the following screenshot:

So, this output shows the number of clusters, points included in that cluster (weight), and the centroid of that cluster.

To view the quality of the cluster, the `qualcluster` command can be used as follows:

```
qualcluster -i / user/hue/SKmeansVec-c /user/hue/SKmeansOut/part-r-
00000-)0 /user/hue/SKmeans-distance.csv
```

- `-i`: This is the vector file
- `-c`: This is the generated cluster
- `-o`: This is the output that will be dumped to the local filesystem

The `qualcluster` command is implemented as the `ClusterQualitySummarizer` class, and it provides descriptive statistics of the cluster quality, such as the average distance in the cluster, the mean, the standard deviation, and so on.

Other than this, it also provides Dunn Index (https://en.wikipedia.org/wiki/Dunn_index) and DaviesBouldinIndex (https://en.wikipedia.org/wiki/Davies%E2%80%93Bouldin_index).

Summary

In this chapter, you learned about `StreamingKMeans` clustering, which is used for streaming data. We discussed both steps involved in this algorithm—streaming and BallKMeans. We used Mahout Streaming K-means on the census1990 data. We also discussed the `clusterQualitySummarizer` class. In the next chapter, we will discuss one more clustering algorithm implemented in Mahout—spectral clustering.

7
Spectral Clustering

In the previous chapters, we discussed the Streaming K-means algorithm and how it is implemented in Apache Mahout. In this chapter, we will discuss one more algorithm implemented in Apache Mahout: spectral clustering.

This algorithm has many applications in the field of machine learning. It is used in the areas of computer vision and speech processing. As the name goes, spectral clustering uses the spectrum of the similarity matrix of data. To assign the clusters, this algorithm considers the correctness of the data in contrast to other clustering algorithms, such as K-means, that considers the compactness of the data. This algorithm is immensely useful in the area of image segmentation. We will discuss the following topics in this chapter:

- Understanding spectral clustering
- Mahout implementation of spectral clustering

Understanding spectral clustering

Clustering applications are across all fields, including, but not limited to, statistics, computer science, and biology. Spectral clustering has a great advantage over traditional clustering algorithms. Results from spectral clustering outperform the traditional clustering algorithms.

Before diving deep into spectral clustering, first let's understand a few mathematical terms used in this concept. More information on all the steps discussed is available in Ulrike von Luxburg's article in Statistics and Computing from December 2007.

Affinity (similarity) graph

While computing the similarity among the given set of points, our goal is to divide the points into groups such that each group has points that are similar. Points in one group have to be dissimilar from points in any other group. The overall goal is to find an affinity matrix from the given set of data. There are several popular graph methods to transform points p1, p2, p3....pn pairwise similarities, or pairwise distance into a graph.

Our aim is to find such a group that satisfies the preceding criteria. We will consider regularly used graphs such as *k-nearest neighbor graph, fully connected graph,* and *the ε-neighborhood graph.*

In the *k-nearest neighbor graph* from a point, x, all other points x_1, x_2, x_3, x_4... will be connected with an edge if all those points are in the radius of the K distance. This can provide the directed graph, but there are ways to make this graph undirected, and one of them is to simply ignore the directions of the edges.

K - nearest neighbor graph

In a fully connected graph, edges are weighted by s_{ij} and points are connected with positive similarity functions. There are many positive similarity functions, such as Gaussian similarity, positive convolution, and so on. The Gaussian similarity function is as follows:

$s(xi, xj) = exp(-||xi - xj||2/(2\ \sigma2))$

Here, the parameter σ controls the width of the neighborhoods. This is the mean distance of samples in the training set.

The *ε-neighborhood graph* is usually considered an unweighted graph. In this graph, we connect points whose pairwise distances are smaller than ε.

Getting graph Laplacian from the affinity matrix

There are different variants of graph Laplacian; based on the situation, one will be selected. To understand the properties of Laplacian graph, knowledge of eigenvalues and eigenvector is also required. So, before further discussing graph Laplacian, let's understand these terms first.

Eigenvectors and eigenvalues

Let's assume that we have an n-dimensional vector with n real values. For example, consider these two two-dimensional vectors:

$$A = \begin{Bmatrix} 2 \\ 4 \end{Bmatrix} \; and \; B = \begin{Bmatrix} -20 \\ -40 \end{Bmatrix}$$

If you notice, we can get vector A from B by multiplying B by (-1/10). So, we can get the following equation :

$$A = \lambda B$$

λ is scalar with value (-1/10). Now, consider the following equation:

$$XU = V$$

Here, X is n*n matrix and U and V are n*1 matrix.

Now, let's assume that U and V are scalar multipliers, as defined in earlier equation. (We can get U by multiplying V by a scalar value). So, we can rewrite the preceding equation as:

$$XU = \lambda U$$

So, U is an eigenvector of matrix X and scalar value λ is the eigenvalue corresponding to the eigenvector. Now, let's take an example to understand how to calculate eigenvector and eigenvalue.

Consider the transformation matrix M as follows:

$$\begin{bmatrix} 4 & 1 \\ 1 & 4 \end{bmatrix}$$

So, as per the discussion earlier, the eigenvector equation will be as follows:

$$MU = \lambda U$$

Rearranging will generate this equation:

$$(M - \lambda I)U = 0$$

Based on this equation, the determinant of $|M - \lambda I|$ is equal to 0. We will calculate this equation as follows:

$$\begin{bmatrix} 4 & 1 \\ 1 & 4 \end{bmatrix} - \lambda \begin{bmatrix} 1 & 0 \\ 0 & 1 \end{bmatrix} = 0$$

This can be simplified as follows:

$$\begin{bmatrix} 4 - \lambda & 1 \\ 1 & 4 - \lambda \end{bmatrix} = 0$$

Based on the determinant calculation, the following equation will emerge:

$$\lambda^2 - 8\lambda + 15 = 0$$

Solving this equation will provide us with two values of λ 3 and 5. Now we can solve the original equation:

$$(M - \lambda I)U = 0$$

With this equation, we will get the eigenvector for eigenvalues 3 and 5:

$$\left(\begin{bmatrix} 4 & 1 \\ 1 & 4 \end{bmatrix} - 3 \begin{bmatrix} 1 & 0 \\ 0 & 1 \end{bmatrix} \right) U = 0$$

Solving this will provide the value for U as $\begin{bmatrix} 1 \\ -1 \end{bmatrix}$.

In a similar way, we will solve the equation for $\lambda = 5$ and get another vector $\begin{bmatrix} 1 \\ 1 \end{bmatrix}$. So, these two vectors are eigenvectors of M.

Now, let's move back to our discussion of the Laplacian graph. For an *unnormalized graph*, the Laplacian Matrix will be calculated as follows:

$$L = D - W$$

Here, D is the degree matrix, which is a diagonal matrix whose (i,i) element is the sum of affinity's matrix ith row. W is the affinity matrix.

As stated by Ulrike von Luxburg in his spectral clustering tutorial, the properties of the unnormalized graph Laplacian are:

- L is symmetric and positive semi-definite
- The smallest eigenvalue of L is 0, the corresponding eigenvector is the constant one vector 1
- L has n non-negative, real-valued eigenvalues $0 = \lambda_1 \le \lambda_2 \le \lambda_3 \cdots \lambda_n$
- Every row sum and column sum of L is zero

The **normalized graph Laplacian matrix** (symmetric) is defined as:

$$L_{sym} = D^{-\frac{1}{2}} L D^{-\frac{1}{2}} = 1 - D^{-\frac{1}{2}} W D^{-\frac{1}{2}}$$

The **normalized graph Laplacian matrix** (random-walk) is defined as:

$$L_{rw} = D^{-1} L = 1 - D^{-1} W$$

Similarly, the spectral clustering tutorial by Ulrike von Luxburg mentions the following properties for a normalized graph Laplacian matrix:

- λ is an eigenvalue of L_{rw} with eigenvector U, if and only if, λ is an eigenvalue of L_{sym} with eigenvector $W = D^{\frac{1}{2}} u$.
- λ is an eigenvalue of L_{rw} with eigenvector U, if and only if, λ and U solve the generalized eigen problem $Lu = \lambda Du$.
- 0 is an eigenvalue of L_{rw} with the constant one vector 1 as eigenvector. 0 is an eigenvalue of L_{sym} with eigenvector $D^{1/2}1$.
- L_{sym} and L_{rw} are positive semi-definite and have n non-negative real-valued eigenvalues $0 = \lambda_1 \le \lambda_2 \le \lambda_3 \cdots \lambda_n$.

Let's take an example to understand the calculation of the Laplacian matrix. Assume that you have the following undirected graph:

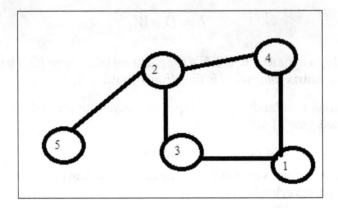

We will calculate the degree matrix and create the adjacency matrix by considering the connectivity of nodes with each other. A degree matrix is a diagonal matrix whose (i,i) element is the sum of ith row of the affinity matrix. Based on the graph, the given degree matrix D will be:

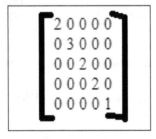

$$\begin{bmatrix} 2 & 0 & 0 & 0 & 0 \\ 0 & 3 & 0 & 0 & 0 \\ 0 & 0 & 2 & 0 & 0 \\ 0 & 0 & 0 & 2 & 0 \\ 0 & 0 & 0 & 0 & 1 \end{bmatrix}$$

The affinity matrix will be:

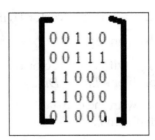

$$\begin{bmatrix} 0 & 0 & 1 & 1 & 0 \\ 0 & 0 & 1 & 1 & 1 \\ 1 & 1 & 0 & 0 & 0 \\ 1 & 1 & 0 & 0 & 0 \\ 0 & 1 & 0 & 0 & 0 \end{bmatrix}$$

Now, using the unnormalized graph Laplacian matrix formula, we can calculate the Laplacian matrix:

$$L = D - W$$

$$\begin{bmatrix} 2 & 0 & -1 & -1 & 0 \\ 0 & 3 & -1 & -1 & -1 \\ -1 & -1 & 2 & 0 & 0 \\ -1 & -1 & 0 & 2 & 0 \\ 0 & -1 & 0 & 0 & -1 \end{bmatrix}$$

The next step would be to find the K eigenvectors of the Laplacian matrix L that correspond to the largest eigenvalues. These K-eigenvectors will be the proxy data of the original dataset and will be passed to the K-means clustering.

The spectral clustering algorithm

We have understood the way we can compute the Laplacian matrix. Based on the choice of the Laplacian matrix, we have available implementation of the spectral clustering algorithm.

Unnormalized spectral clustering:

*   Input for this clustering will be the similarity matrix and the number K, of clusters to construct.
*   A weighted adjacency matrix W will be calculated. In this algorithm, the unnormalized graph Laplacian will be computed.
*   Next, the first k eigenvectors of Laplacian matrix will be computed.
*   Now, let's consider a matrix of size n*k (similarity matrix was of size n*n); it has K eigenvectors as columns. Now, consider each row of this matrix as vector and cluster the points using K-means.
*   The output will be the resulting cluster.

Normalized spectral clustering

Based on the choice of the normalized graph Laplacian matrix symmetric or random walk, two more implementations of spectral clustering are available. One uses the symmetric Laplacian graph, as defined in *Normalized Cuts and Image Segmentation, IEEE Transactions on Pattern Analysis and Machine Intelligence, Jainbo Shi* and *Jitendra Malik (2000)*. The other one uses the random walk Laplacian matrix to compute the spectral clustering, as defined in the paper *On spectral clustering, Analysis and an algorithm, Andrew Y. Ng, Michael I. Jordan, Yair Weiss (2002)*. It can be defined as:

- Input for this clustering will be the similarity matrix and the number k, of clusters to construct.
- A weighted adjacency matrix, W, will be calculated. In this algorithm, a normalized graph Laplacian will be computed $\left(L_{sym} \right)$.
- Next, the first K eigenvectors of the Laplacian matrix will be computed.
- Now, let's consider a matrix U of size n*k (similarity matrix was of size n*n) that has K eigenvectors as columns.
- Create a new matrix M, from the earlier one, normalizing the rows to norm 1:

$$m_{ij} = u_{ij} / \sum_{k} u_{ik}^2$$

- Now, consider each row of this matrix as a vector and cluster the points using K-means.
- The output will be the resulting cluster.

Now that we have understood the streaming algorithm in general, let's move on to discussing how Mahout has implemented this algorithm.

Mahout implementation of spectral clustering

The Mahout implementation of spectral clustering requires an affinity matrix as the input from the user, and it uses the K-means algorithm for the final clustering. Usually, Mahout clustering consists of the following steps:

1. User takes a matrix of k*n-dimensional data to which he wants to cluster.
2. User will have to create a similarity matrix from the original data matrix. This will be a k*k transformation of the original matrix based on how the points are related to each other.

3. From the similarity matrix, an affinity matrix needs to be created. Mahout takes a type of Hadoop-backed affinity matrix as an input in the form of a text file. This is a weighted, undirected graph. Each line of a text file represents a single directional edge between two nodes. Each line consists of three comma separated values. The first value corresponds to the source node, second to the destination node, and third to the weight. As per the matrix, it will be represented as row index i, column index j, and the value: i, j, value.

   The affinity matrix is symmetric, and any unspecified i, j pair will be considered as 0.

   As mentioned, as of now, we will have to provide an affinity matrix as an input, but there is an open JIRA for future release, after which the creation of an affinity matrix will be a part of the algorithm. More details can be found at MAHOUT-1539 Implement affinity matrix computation in Mahout DSL.

   The affinity matrix can be contained in a single text file or span many text files, but as per MAHOUT-978, the file name cannot have a prefix, such as a leading underscore _ or period .. .

4. The `AffinityMatrixInputJob` class under the `org.apache.mahout.clustering.spectral` package reads the affinity matrix file and provides fully-populated and initialized `DistributedRowMatrix`, a FileSystem-backed VectorIterable in which the vectors live in a `SequenceFile<WritableCompa rable,VectorWritable>`, and distributed operations are executed as M/R passes on Hadoop.

5. Now, an internally diagonal matrix is created using `MatrixDiagonalizeJob`. Basically, it returns a vector whose i_th element is the sum of all the elements in the i_th row of the original matrix.

6. Mahout will use the normalized L_{sym} Laplacian matrix calculation.

7. To convert the eigenvector matrix to unit rows, Mahout has `UnitVectorizerJob`. As per the class file comment, this job normalizes each row to a unit vector length. If the input is a matrix U, and the output is a matrix W, the job follows:

   *v_ij = u_ij / sqrt(sum_j(u_ij * u_ij))*

   http://archive.cloudera.com/cdh5/cdh/5/mahout/mahout-core/org/
   apache/mahout/clustering/spectral/UnitVectorizerJob.html

8. `VectorMatrixMultiplicationJob` multiplies the diagonal matrix with the affinity matrix.

9. The main class that triggers the jobs is the `SpectralKMeansDriver` class.

We will run a few examples to see how to run `spectralkmeans` in Mahout. We will take the data for the affinity matrix from http://danbri.org/2011/mahout/afftest.txt (as mentioned in mahout jira-MAHOUT-524). This data will appear as shown in the following figure:

```
1,6,1.0
2,6,1.0
3,6,1.0
4,6,1.0
5,20,1.0
6,1,1.0
6,2,1.0
6,3,1.0
6,4,1.0
6,9,1.0
6,11,1.0
6,12,1.0
6,13,1.0
6,14,1.0
6,20,1.0
7,12,1.0
7,32,1.0
8,9,1.0
```

10. We will put this file into HDFS using the following command:

```
bin/hadoopfs -put /user/hue/Affinitymat.csv
/user/hue/SpectralclusterInput
```

11. Now, we will use the following command to run `SpectralKmeans` clustering:

```
bin/mahoutspectralkmeans -k 2 -
i/user/hue/SpectralclusterInput/   -o
/user/hue/SpectralCluster-maxIter10 --dimensions 38
```

In this command:

- `k`: This refers to the number of clusters AND number of top eigenvectors to use
- `i`: This refers to the input location of the affinity matrix directory
- `o`: This refers to the output directory
- `maxIter`: This refers to the maximum number of K-means iterations
- `dimensions`: This refers to the number of data points

```
[root@sandbox ~]# mahout spectralkmeans -i /user/hue/SpectralclusterInput -o /user/hue/SpectralCluster/ -k 2 -x 10 --dimensions 37
MAHOUT_LOCAL is not set; adding HADOOP_CONF_DIR to classpath.
Running on hadoop, using /usr/lib/hadoop/bin/hadoop and HADOOP_CONF_DIR=/etc/hadoop/conf
MAHOUT-JOB: /usr/lib/mahout/mahout-examples-0.9.0.2.1.1.0-385-job.jar
15/07/05 08:40:38 WARN driver.MahoutDriver: No spectralkmeans.props found on classpath, will use command-line arguments only
15/07/05 08:40:41 INFO common.AbstractJob: Command line arguments: [--clusters=[2], --convergenceDelta=[0.5], --dimensions=[37], --distanceMeasure=[org.apache.mahout.co
mmon.distance.SquaredEuclideanDistanceMeasure], --endPhase=[2147483647], --input=[/user/hue/SpectralclusterInput], --maxIter=[10], --outerProdBlockHeight=[30000], --out
put=[/user/hue/SpectralCluster/], --oversampling=[15], --powerIter=[0], --reduceTasks=[10], --startPhase=[0], --tempDir=[temp]]
15/07/05 08:40:46 INFO client.RMProxy: Connecting to ResourceManager at sandbox.hortonworks.com/10.0.2.15:8050
15/07/05 08:40:48 WARN mapreduce.JobSubmitter: Hadoop command-line option parsing not performed. Implement the Tool interface and execute your application with ToolRunn
er to remedy this.
15/07/05 08:40:55 INFO input.FileInputFormat: Total input paths to process : 1
15/07/05 08:40:55 INFO mapreduce.JobSubmitter: number of splits:1
15/07/05 08:40:56 INFO mapreduce.JobSubmitter: Submitting tokens for job: job_1436106423421_0001
15/07/05 08:40:59 INFO impl.YarnClientImpl: Submitted application application_1436106423421_0001
15/07/05 08:40:59 INFO mapreduce.Job: The url to track the job: http://sandbox.hortonworks.com:8088/proxy/application_1436106423421_0001/
15/07/05 08:40:59 INFO mapreduce.Job: Running job: job_1436106423421_0001
15/07/05 08:41:37 INFO mapreduce.Job: Job job_1436106423421_0001 running in uber mode : false
15/07/05 08:41:38 INFO mapreduce.Job:  map 0% reduce 0%
15/07/05 08:42:03 INFO mapreduce.Job:  map 100% reduce 0%
15/07/05 08:42:25 INFO mapreduce.Job:  map 100% reduce 100%
15/07/05 08:42:26 INFO mapreduce.Job: Job job_1436106423421_0001 completed successfully
15/07/05 08:42:27 INFO mapreduce.Job: Counters: 49
        File System Counters
                FILE: Number of bytes read=2690
                FILE: Number of bytes written=204887
                FILE: Number of read operations=0
                FILE: Number of large read operations=0
                FILE: Number of write operations=0
                HDFS: Number of bytes read=1438
                HDFS: Number of bytes written=1750
                HDFS: Number of read operations=6
                HDFS: Number of large read operations=0
                HDFS: Number of write operations=2
```

12. Once the job is finished in the output folder, you can see folders for
    kmeans _out and for part-eigenSeed as well. You can review the content
    of the file with the following command:

    bin/mahoutseqdumper -i /user/hue/SpectralCluster/clusters-0/part-eigenSeed -o /tmp/output

The kmeans_out folder is similar to the one we got in the K-means clustering. To view
the output, run the following command:

**bin/mahout clusterdump -i
/user/hue/SpectralCluster/kmeans_out/clusters-1-final -o
/user/hue/specclusterdumpout.txt -dtsequencefile --pointsDir
/user/hue/SpectralCluster/kmeans_out/clusteredPoints**

```
[root@sandbox ~]# mahout clusterdump -i /user/hue/SpectralCluster/kmeans_out/clusters-1-final -o /user/hue/specclusterdumpout.txt -dt sequencefile --pointsDir /user/hue
/SpectralCluster/kmeans_out/clusteredPoints
MAHOUT_LOCAL is not set; adding HADOOP_CONF_DIR to classpath.
Running on hadoop, using /usr/lib/hadoop/bin/hadoop and HADOOP_CONF_DIR=/etc/hadoop/conf
MAHOUT-JOB: /usr/lib/mahout/mahout-examples-0.9.0.2.1.1.0-385-job.jar
15/07/05 10:25:58 INFO common.AbstractJob: Command line arguments: {--dictionaryType=[sequencefile], --distanceMeasure=[org.apache.mahout.common.distance.SquaredEuclide
anDistanceMeasure], --endPhase=[2147483647], --input=[/user/hue/SpectralCluster/kmeans_out/clusters-1-final], --output=[/user/hue/specclusterdumpout.txt], --outputForma
t=[TEXT], --pointsDir=[/user/hue/SpectralCluster/kmeans_out/clusteredPoints], --startPhase=[0], --tempDir=[temp]}
15/07/05 10:26:06 INFO clustering.ClusterDumper: Wrote 2 clusters
```

The output will provide information about the cluster center, radius, and the points in that cluster. It will look like the following:

```
{n=24 c=[0.928, 0.020] r=[0.210, 0.307]}
    weight : [props - optional]:  Point:
    1.0 : [distance=0.006382068877685887]: 0 = [1.000, -0.015]
    1.0 : [distance=0.01766217314100471]: 1 = [0.996, -0.094]
    1.0 : [distance=0.01766217314100471]: 2 = [0.996, -0.094]
    1.0 : [distance=0.01766217314100471]: 3 = [0.996, -0.094]
    1.0 : [distance=0.01766217314100471]: 4 = [0.996, -0.094]
    1.0 : [distance=0.49185752456223275]: 5 = [0.752, -0.659]
    1.0 : [distance=0.007839857409958517]: 7 = [0.997, 0.075]
    1.0 : [distance=0.01893190280838608]: 8 = [0.995, -0.100]
    1.0 : [distance=0.007421926366014242]: 10 = [0.997, 0.071]
    1.0 : [distance=0.18818935889942545]: 11 = [0.892, 0.453]
    1.0 : [distance=0.007580412482251608]: 15 = [1.000, -0.029]
    1.0 : [distance=0.007421926366014242]: 16 = [0.997, 0.071]
    1.0 : [distance=0.0068932307928766626]: 18 = [0.998, 0.065]
    1.0 : [distance=1.8641302021339248]: 20 = [-0.023, 1.000]
    1.0 : [distance=0.006557849605056454]: 21 = [0.998, 0.061]
    1.0 : [distance=0.005340447754238475]: 22 = [0.999, 0.036]
    1.0 : [distance=0.07862044480371666]: 23 = [0.954, 0.299]
    1.0 : [distance=0.49185752456223275]: 27 = [0.752, -0.659]
    1.0 : [distance=0.024807285514032884]: 29 = [0.986, 0.167]
    1.0 : [distance=0.011702102940353454]: 30 = [0.994, 0.106]
    1.0 : [distance=0.006910281717172013165]: 35 = [1.000, -0.022]
    1.0 : [distance=0.006910281717172013165]: 36 = [1.000, -0.022]
    1.0 : [distance=0.006910281717172013165]: 37 = [1.000, -0.022]
{n=16 c=[-0.064, -0.837] r=[0.488, 0.240]}
```

We run this algorithm with a few parameters, but, actually, we can provide more parameters to calculate spectralKMeans. The full list of parameters is as follows:

```
[--input<input> --output <output> --dimensions <dimensions> --
clusters
<clusters> --distanceMeasure<distanceMeasure> --convergenceDelta
<convergenceDelta> --maxIter<maxIter> --overwrite --usessvd --
reduceTasks
<reduceTasks> --outerProdBlockHeight<outerProdBlockHeight> --
oversampling
<oversampling> --powerIter<powerIter> --help --tempDir<tempDir> --
startPhase
<startPhase> --endPhase<endPhase>]
```

This can be viewed by typing the bin/mahout spectralkmeans command.

If you notice the input parameters, you will find a parameter named usessvd. This parameter informs the algorithm to use **Stochastic Singular Value Decomposition (SSVD)** for dimensionality reduction. More information on this can be found at https://en.wikipedia.org/wiki/Singular_value_decomposition.

Mahout-specific details can be found at http://mahout.apache.org/users/dim-reduction/ssvd.html.

Summary

In this chapter, we discussed `SpectralKMeans` clustering and the steps involved in running this algorithm. We discussed different flavors of the algorithm and the one that Mahout has implemented. We also covered the different classes that Mahout has provided to implement SpectralKmeans clustering. We executed a small example and discussed the output. The Mahout community is working on this algorithm, and we will see a lot of new changes in this algorithm in upcoming releases. Follow the Apache Mahout link for more information on new features of `SpectralKmeans` clustering. In the next chapter, we will discuss how to improve cluster quality.

8
Improving Cluster Quality

In the previous chapters, we discussed different clustering techniques and techniques available in Mahout. In this chapter, we will focus on how to evaluate whether our algorithm has performed well or not. First, we will have to understand how our cluster is working, and then we can see where we can improve our cluster. The output of the clustering algorithm is affected by the algorithm, input parameters, and other parameters. The basic idea behind improving cluster quality is to change different parameters, such as the distance measure or input matrix, or check the other parameters that are passed to the input algorithms. So, while we evaluate the cluster, we basically perform the following tasks:

- Measuring cluster quality
- Finding the number of clusters in the given dataset
- Finding out how changing distance measure can affect the cluster quality

We will discuss the following topics in this chapter:

- Evaluating clusters
- Improving cluster quality

Evaluating clusters

Cluster evaluation involves cluster validation. We can apply multiple algorithms to get the clustering results, and we wish to know how one result is better than the other.

Two types of methods are available to evaluate clusters:

- Extrinsic methods
- Intrinsic methods

Let's take a look at each of these types.

Extrinsic methods

Extrinsic methods are the methods in which data that is not used for clustering is used for evaluation. This data consists of known class labels and external benchmarks. These benchmarks are thought of as gold standards and are often created by experts. A measure on clustering quality is effective if it satisfies the following four criteria (*A comparison of Extrinsic Clustering Evaluation Metrics based on Formal constraints, Enrique Amigó, Julio Gonzalo, Javier Artiles,* and *FelisaVerdejo*):

- **Cluster Homogeneity**: Clusters should not mix items belonging to different categories. Look at the following diagram:

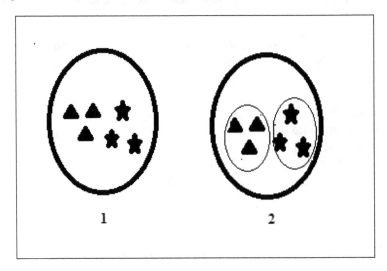

Cluster 1 has all six data points in one cluster, while cluster 2 divides six points into two clusters based on shapes. So, the quality of cluster 2 is better than that of cluster 1.

- **Cluster Completeness**: The second criterion is cluster completeness, which is basically the counterpart of the first one. Different clusters should contain items from different clusters.

- **Rag Bag**: Sometimes we find objects that cannot be merged with any of the available categories. This rag bag category is often called miscellaneous or others. A perfect clustering system should identify these objects and put them into a different set of categories. So, we can have something like clean clusters and one cluster with noisy objects.

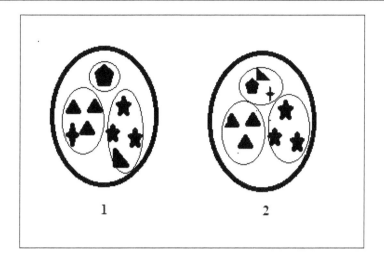

1   2

Cluster 1 has three clusters, but noise objects are included in each cluster. On the other hand, cluster 2, which also has three clusters, has two clean clusters and one cluster with different (all other) objects. So, cluster 2 is of higher quality than cluster 1.

- **Cluster size versus quantity**: A large number of small errors in a small cluster are not preferable. Instead, small errors in big cluster are preferable. Splitting a large cluster into smaller categories is less harmful than splitting a small cluster into a smaller cluster.

Some of the quality measuring techniques of clustering algorithm using extrinsic methods include:

- **Jaccard index**: The Jaccard index is used to quantify the similarity between two datasets. This index takes a value between 0 and 1. The value 1 indicates that two datasets are the same, and 0 indicates that there is no common element in the dataset. The Jaccard index is defined by following formula:

$$B$$
$$A$$

$$B$$
$$A$$

$$J(A,B) =$$

It can be explained as the number of unique elements in both the datasets divided by the total number of unique elements in the datasets. It can also be explained as follows:

$$\frac{TruePositive}{TruePositive + FalsePositive + FalseNegative}$$

- **Rand statistics**: Rand statistics is the measurement of the percentage of correct decisions made by the algorithm. Rand statistics computation informs how similar clusters are with the benchmark classification. Rand statistics can be calculated as follows:

$$\frac{TruePositive + TrueNegative}{TruePositive + FalsePositive + FalseNegative + TrueNegative}$$

- **F-measure**: The Rand measure has a problem — it provides equal weightage to both false positive and false negative. F-measure is used to balance the false negative contribution through a parameter, $\beta \geq 0$. It can be calculated as follows:

$$\frac{\left(\beta^2 + 1\right) * P * R}{\left(\beta^2\right) * P + R}$$

Here, P and R are called precision and recall rate.

- **Fowlkes-Mallows index (FM)**: Mathematically, the Fowlkes-Mallows index is the geometric mean of precision and recall. Fowlkes-Mallow calculates the similarity between the classification benchmark and clusters returned by the algorithm. Higher values indicate that clusters and benchmark classification are similar. It is calculated as per the following formula:

$$\sqrt{\frac{\dfrac{TruePositive}{TruePositive + FalsePositive} * TruePositive}{TruePositive + FalseNegative}}$$

- **Entropy-based cluster evaluation**: The entropy of a cluster indicates how different categories are distributed within each cluster. The smaller the entropy, the better the clustering performance. The following formula is used to compute it:

$$-\sum_{k=0}^{n} P(L_i) * log_2 \left(P(L_i) \right)$$

Here, $P(L_i)$ is the probability of the element from category i from cluster L.

Now, let's take a look at some intrinsic methods.

Intrinsic methods

Intrinsic methods help to evaluate a cluster by examining the compactness of the cluster and separation of the clusters. When situations where one clustering algorithm performs better than the other, intrinsic methods provide good insights. The following methods are used to measure the quality of a cluster under intrinsic methods:

- **Dunn Index**: The Dunn index is helpful in the case where clusters are dense and well separated from each other. It can be defined mathematically as:

  Minimum inter-cluster distance/maximum intra-cluster distance

  Let's take a look at inter-cluster and intra-cluster distances.

- **Inter-cluster**: This distance is the distance between the centroid of the clusters. We use some distance measure to calculate the distance between the clusters. Look at the following figure to understand inter-cluster distance:

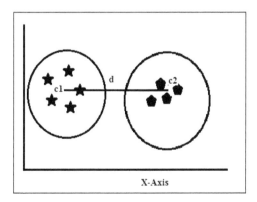

The points *c1* and *c2* represent the centroid of two clusters, and *d* is the distance between them. Using the following code, we can calculate inter-cluster distance using Mahout (the code is the same as the one provided in Mahout in Action with a small change):

Import statements:

```
import java.util.ArrayList;
import java.util.List;
import org.apache.hadoop.conf.Configuration;
import org.apache.hadoop.fs.FileSystem;
import org.apache.hadoop.fs.Path;
import org.apache.hadoop.io.SequenceFile;
import org.apache.hadoop.io.Writable;
import org.apache.mahout.clustering.Cluster;
import org.apache.mahout.clustering.iterator.ClusterWritable;
import
org.apache.mahout.common.distance.CosineDistanceMeasure;
import org.apache.mahout.common.distance.DistanceMeasure;
```

Method:

```
public void printClusterDistance() throws Exception{
  String clusterLocation = "<your hdfs location of
    clustered data (KMeanscluster/clusters-4/
      part-r-00000)>";
  Path path = new Path(clusterLocation);
  FileSystemfs =
    FileSystem.get(path.toUri(),getConfiguration());
  List<Cluster> clusters = new ArrayList<Cluster>();
  SequenceFile.Reader reader = new
    SequenceFile.Reader(fs,path,getConfiguration());
  Writable key = (Writable)
    reader.getKeyClass().newInstance();
  Writable value = (Writable)
    reader.getValueClass().newInstance();
  while (reader.next(key, value)) {
    ClusterWritable cluster = (ClusterWritable) value;
    clusters.add(cluster.getValue());
    value = (Writable)
      reader.getValueClass().newInstance();
}
DistanceMeasure measure = new CosineDistanceMeasure();
double max = 0;
double min = Double.MAX_VALUE;
double sum = 0;
int count = 0;
```

```
for (int i = 0; i<clusters.size(); i++) {
  for (int j = i + 1; j <clusters.size(); j++) {
    double d = measure.distance
      (clusters.get(i).getCenter(),
    clusters.get(j).getCenter());
    min = Math.min(d, min);
    max = Math.max(d, max);
    sum += d;
    count++;
  }
}
  System.out.println
    ("Maximum Inter-cluster Distance: " + max);
  System.out.println
    ("Minimum Inter-cluster Distance: " + min);
  System.out.println
    ("Average Inter-cluster Distance(Scaled): "
    + (sum / count - min) / (max - min));

}
```

After running this code, you can view the output as follows:

```
Maximum Inter-cluster Distance: 0.22206337540229804
Minimum Inter-cluster Distance: 0.022657738419520124
Average Inter-cluster Distance(Scaled): 0.3687703331905521
```

- **Intra-cluster distance**: This represents the distance between the members of a cluster. It shows how close the points are to each other in a cluster.

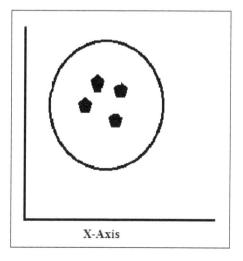

X-Axis

The Dunn index can be represented as follows:

$$\frac{min_{1 \le i \le n} c(i, j)}{max_{1 < k < n} c'(k)}$$

Here, c (i,j) is the distance between cluster i and j, and $c'(k)$ is the intra-cluster distance of cluster k.

Clustering algorithms that produce a high Dunn index are preferred. (For more information on the Dunn index, visit https://en.wikipedia.org/wiki/Dunn_index).

- **Davies-Bouldin index**: Another index of the intrinsic method is the Davies-Bouldin index. It is calculated based on the following formula:

$$1/n \sum_{i=1}^{n} \max_{j \ne i} \left(\frac{\sigma_i + \sigma_j}{d(c_i, c_j)} \right)$$

Here, n is the number of clusters, c_i is the centroid of the cluster i, and $d(c_i, c_j)$ is the distance between centroids. σ_i is the average distance of all the points in cluster i to its centroid.

The algorithm that produces a collection of clusters and has the smallest value in terms of the Davies-Bouldin index is considered the best algorithm. For more information on the Davies-Bouldin index, visit https://en.wikipedia.org/wiki/Davies%E2%80%93Bouldin_index.

- **Silhouette coefficient**: This index is used well with K-means clustering algorithms to determine the optimal number of clusters. It provides a graphical representation of how well each element lies within a cluster. To calculate the silhouette coefficient, for each point, find the average distance between the point and all other points in the same cluster and call this *A(i)*. Now, find the average distance between each point and all points in the nearest cluster and call this *B(i)*. The silhouette coefficient of this point will be computed using the following formula:

$$A(i), B(i)$$
$$max$$
$$\underline{B(i) - A(i)}$$

Calculation will be done for each point, and the average cluster coefficient will be calculated. A graph between the number of clusters and coefficient value will be calculated, and the higher value of coefficient will be selected. (`https://en.wikipedia.org/wiki/Silhouette_(clustering)`)

The value of coefficient is between -1 and 1. The smaller the value, the more compact the cluster.

Using DistanceMeasure interface

Usually, the quality of cluster depends on the selected distance measure and the weight of the features in the vector (document). A correct distance measure can bring similar items together. Mahout provides us the flexibility to write custom distance measures. Mahout provides the DistanceMeasure interface under `org. apache.mahout.common.distance` package. The main method to override here is `doubledistance(Vector v1, Vector v2)`.

Let's take a look at a small implementation of this interface in the following code snippet (source: Mahout in Action):

```
public double distance(Vector vector1, Vector vector2) {
    if(vector1.size()!=vector2.size()){
    throw newCardinalityException(vector1.size(), vector2.size());

}
    double lengthSquaredv1 = vector1.getLengthSquared();
    double lengthSquaredv2 = vector2.getLengthSquared();
    double dotProduct = vector2.dot(vector1);
    double denominator = Math.sqrt(lengthSquaredv1)*
      Math.sqrt(lengthSquaredv2);
    if (denominator <dotProduct) {
      denominator = dotProduct;
    }
    double distance = 1.0 - dotProduct / denominator;
    if (distance < 0.5) {
      return (1 - distance) * (distance * distance)
```

```
        + distance * Math.sqrt(distance);
    } else return Math.sqrt(distance);
}
```

Now, create the jar of this code and put it into the local directory. For command line uses, before running your clustering algorithm command, run the following command:

export HADOOP_CLASSPATH=<path to jar file>

While providing the option for –dm, provide the full name of the class:
`Packagename.classname`

Summary

In this chapter, we discussed how to improve cluster quality. We looked at different measuring techniques that help us to identify cluster quality. We further discussed intrinsic and extrinsic methods for cluster evaluation techniques. Then, we saw how to use inter-cluster distance measure to calculate the Dunn index. We also discussed custom distance measure in Mahout. A wrong selection of distance measure can affect the quality of clusters badly. In the next, and final, chapter of this book, we will use Hadoop to run our clustering job and see how to go for clustering in production.

9
Creating a Cluster Model for Production

We have visited the different clustering algorithms offered by Mahout. We have also discussed how to use these algorithms with different datasets. We saw how to evaluate and improve cluster qualities. Now, in this final chapter, we will evaluate how to create a production-ready clustering model.

In this chapter, we will pick up one real-world scenario and discuss the following points:

- Preparing the dataset
- Launching the Mahout job on the cluster
- Performance tuning for the job

Preparing the dataset

The dataset preparation is the most important task of any machine learning related activity. You are not going to get text or structured data in all use cases. Collecting the data in the system where you are applying an algorithm is an interesting task. Data can be collected using different ways, such as:

- Pulling the data from the relational database to the Hadoop cluster (using Apache Sqoop)
- Continuously streaming data into Hadoop. The Hadoop ecosystem provides lots of way to do this, examples include Flume, storm, and so on
- Other ways include getting data using ftp, and so on

For example, in this chapter, we will pick up the use case where we will get a continuous stream of data into our system. We will take up the use case from Twitter. Based on tweets from the users, we will try to cluster similar users together. In a real-world production scenario, we will use one of the available technologies in the Hadoop ecosystem to collect a live stream of tweets (we can select Flume as part of the exercise).

I strongly recommend you to have a look at it to understand how to use flume to collect Twitter streams. There are online resources available for this. For example, http://blog.hubacek.uk/streaming-tweets-into-hadoop-part-ii/.

Here, we will use the following piece of code to collect 200000 tweets from Twitter using the Twitter4J API:

```
//Import statements:
importjava.io.BufferedWriter;
importjava.io.FileWriter;
importjava.io.IOException;
importjava.io.PrintWriter;
import twitter4j.StallWarning;
import twitter4j.Status;
import twitter4j.StatusDeletionNotice;
import twitter4j.StatusListener;
import twitter4j.TwitterStream;
import twitter4j.TwitterStreamFactory;
import twitter4j.conf.ConfigurationBuilder;

//This is the class used to collect the desired number of tweets:

public class TweetsCollector {
  private class ExampleListener implements StatusListener {
    long count = 0;
    static final long maxCount = 200000; /* Number of tweets you
    want to collect.*/
    PrintWriter out;
    TwitterStream tweetStream;

    ExampleListener (TwitterStreamts) throws IOException {
      tweetStream = ts;
      out = new PrintWriter(new BufferedWriter(new
      FileWriter("\\user\\hue\\Tweets\\tweets.txt")));
    }

    public void onStatus(Status status) {
      String username = status.getUser().getScreenName();
```

```
      String text = status.getText().replace('\n', ' ');
      out.println(username + "\t" + text);
      System.out.println(username + "\t" + text);
      count++;
      if(count >= maxCount) {
        tweetStream.shutdown();
        out.close();
      }
    }

    @Override
    public void onDeletionNotice(StatusDeletionNotice arg0) {
      // TODO Auto-generated method stub

    }

    @Override
    public void onException(Exception arg0) {
      // TODO Auto-generated method stub

    }


    @Override
    public void onTrackLimitationNotice(int arg0) {
      // TODO Auto-generated method stub

    }

    @Override
    public void onScrubGeo(long arg0, long arg1) {
      // TODO Auto-generated method stub

    }

    @Override
    public void onStallWarning(StallWarning arg0) {
      // TODO Auto-generated method stub

    }
}

StatusListenermakeListener(TwitterStreamts) throws IOException {
  returnthis.newExampleListener(ts);
```

```
    }

    public static void main(String[] args) throws IOException {
        ConfigurationBuildercb = new ConfigurationBuilder();
        cb.setDebugEnabled(true).setOAuthConsumerKey("*********")
        .setOAuthConsumerSecret("***********")
        .setOAuthAccessToken("******************")
        .setOAuthAccessTokenSecret("***************");
        TwitterStreamFactorytf= new TwitterStreamFactory(cb.build());
        TwitterStreamtwitterStream =tf.getInstance();
        TweetsCollector td = new TweetsCollector();
        StatusListener listener = td.makeListener(twitterStream);
        twitterStream.addListener(listener);
        twitterStream.sample();
    }
}
```

You can only run this code if you have your own private account. After you obtain `ConsumerKey`, `ConsumerSecret`, `AccessToken`, and `AccessTokenSecret` from `https://dev.twitter.com/apps`, follow these steps:

1. Browse the page at `https://dev.twitter.com/apps`

2. Create an account if you do not already have one and sign in; this will show you the following screen:

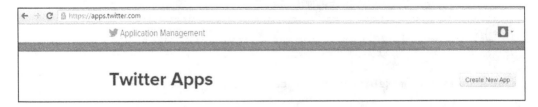

3. Click on **Create New App**, fill in the details, and sign the following agreement.

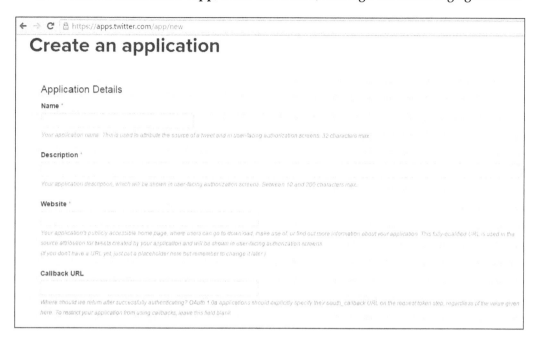

4. Once the application is created, you will see these four tabs on the next screen:

5. Click on the **Keys and Access Tokens** tab, and you will find **ConsumerKey** and **ConsumerSecret** under **Application Settings**. Then, clicking on **Token Action** will generate **AccessToken** and **AccessTokenSecret**.

We know, from previous chapters, that we will have to convert this data into a Mahout-readable format. We will convert this data into a sequence file and convert this to vectors understandable by Mahout. We can convert these sequence files using the `mapreduce` program. In the mapper, the username will be treated as the key, tweets by this will be values, and they will be passed to the reducer. The reducer will output the username as key, all tweets by a particular user as values, and this output will be converted as sequence files.

The following is the `mapreduce` program to convert to sequence files:

```
Imports
importjava.io.IOException;
importorg.apache.hadoop.conf.Configuration;
importorg.apache.hadoop.conf.Configured;
importorg.apache.hadoop.fs.Path;
importorg.apache.hadoop.io.ByteWritable;
importorg.apache.hadoop.io.BytesWritable;
importorg.apache.hadoop.io.LongWritable;
importorg.apache.hadoop.io.Text;
importorg.apache.hadoop.mapreduce.lib.input.TextInputFormat;
import org.apache.hadoop.mapreduce.lib.output.
SequenceFileOutputFormat;
importorg.apache.hadoop.mapreduce.Job;
importorg.apache.hadoop.mapreduce.Mapper;
importorg.apache.hadoop.mapreduce.Reducer;
importorg.apache.hadoop.mapreduce.lib.input.FileInputFormat;
importorg.apache.hadoop.mapreduce.lib.output.FileOutputFormat;
importorg.apache.hadoop.util.GenericOptionsParser;
importorg.apache.hadoop.util.Tool;
importorg.apache.hadoop.util.ToolRunner;


// Class with mapper, reducer and driver
public class TweetsByUsers extends Configured implements Tool {
  public static class UserAsKeyMapper extends
    Mapper<LongWritable,Text,Text,Text>{
    protectedvoid map(LongWritable key, Text value,Context
      context) throwsIOException, InterruptedException {
      String[] fields = value.toString().split("\t");
      if (fields.length - 1 < 1 ||fields.length - 1 < 0) {
        context.getCounter("Map",
        "LinesWithErrors").increment(1);
        return;
      }
      String userName = fields[0];
      String tweet = fields[1];
      context.write(new Text(userName), new Text(tweet));
    }

  }

  public static class UserAsKeyReducer extends Reducer<Text, Text,
    Text, BytesWritable>{
```

```
  protectedvoid reduce(Text key, Iterable<Text>values,Context
    context) throwsIOException,InterruptedException {
  StringBuilder output = newStringBuilder();
  for (Text value : values) {
    output.append(value.toString()).append(" ");
    }
    context.write(key,
      newBytesWritable(output.toString().trim().getBytes()));
  }

}

publicint run(String[] args) throwsIOException {
  Configuration conf = newConfiguration();
  conf.addResource(new Path("/etc/hadoop/conf/core-site.xml"));
  conf.addResource(new Path("/etc/hadoop/conf/hdfs-site.xml"));
  conf.addResource(new Path("/etc/hadoop/conf/mapred-site.xml"));
  conf.addResource(new Path("/etc/hadoop/conf/yarn-site.xml"));
  String[] otherArgs = newGenericOptionsParser
    (conf, args).getRemainingArgs();
  if (otherArgs.length != 2) {
    System.err.println("Usage: input and output <in><out>");
    System.exit(2);
  }
  Job job = Job.getInstance(conf,"TweetsByUser");
  job.setJarByClass(TweetsByUsers.class);
  job.setMapperClass(UserAsKeyMapper.class);
  job.setReducerClass(UserAsKeyReducer.class);
  job.setMapOutputKeyClass(Text.class);
  job.setMapOutputValueClass(Text.class);
  job.setInputFormatClass(TextInputFormat.class);
  job.setOutputFormatClass(SequenceFileOutputFormat.class);
  job.setOutputKeyClass(Text.class);
  job.setOutputValueClass(ByteWritable.class);
  Path outputPath = newPath(otherArgs[1]);
  FileInputFormat.addInputPath(job,new Path(otherArgs[0]));
  FileOutputFormat.setOutputPath(job, outputPath);
  outputPath.getFileSystem(conf).delete(outputPath, true);
  try {
    return(job.waitForCompletion(true) ? 0 : 1);
  }
  catch (ClassNotFoundException | InterruptedException e) {

    e.printStackTrace();
```

```
        return 0;
    }

  publicstaticvoid main(String[] args) throws Exception {
    intexitCode = ToolRunner.run(newTweetsByUsers(), args);
    System.exit(exitCode);
    }
}
```

Before applying the TF-IDF feature weighting technique, we will have to remove the stop words. We should change alternate spellings using a phonetic filter. These filters are implemented in the codec library. The following is one of the implementations of Analyzer:

```
Imports:
importjava.io.IOException;
importjava.io.Reader;
importjava.io.StringReader;
importorg.apache.commons.codec.language.DoubleMetaphone;
importorg.apache.lucene.analysis.Analyzer;
importorg.apache.lucene.analysis.TokenStream;
importorg.apache.lucene.analysis.Tokenizer;
importorg.apache.lucene.analysis.core.StopFilter;
importorg.apache.lucene.analysis.core.WhitespaceTokenizer;
importorg.apache.lucene.analysis.en.PorterStemFilter;
importorg.apache.lucene.analysis.standard.StandardAnalyzer;
importorg.apache.lucene.analysis.standard.StandardTokenizer;
importorg.apache.lucene.analysis.tokenattributes.CharTermAttribut;
importorg.apache.lucene.util.Version;

//Class extending Analyzer
public class TweetsAnalyzer extends Analyzer {
  privateDoubleMetaphone filter = new DoubleMetaphone();

  @Override
  protectedTokenStreamComponentscreateComponents
    (String arg0, Reader reader) {
    Tokenizer source;

    finalTokenStream result = new PorterStemFilter
      (new StopFilter(Version.LUCENE_CURRENT,
        new StandardTokenizer(Version.LUCENE_CURRENT, reader),
      StandardAnalyzer.STOP_WORDS_SET));
    CharTermAttributetermAtt = (CharTermAttribute)
      result.addAttribute(CharTermAttribute.class);
```

```
      StringBuilderbuf = new StringBuilder();
      try {
        while (result.incrementToken()) {
          String word = new String(termAtt.buffer(), 0,
            termAtt.length());
          buf.append(filter.encode(word)).append(" ");}
        }
        catch (IOException e) {
          e.printStackTrace();
      }
      source =  new WhitespaceTokenizer(Version.LUCENE_CURRENT,
        new StringReader(buf.toString()));
      return new TokenStreamComponents(source);
    }


  }
```

Now, we can use the following command to use this analyzer in our code:

```
bin/mahout seq2sparse  --maxNGramSize 2 -minLLR 20 -maxDFPercent 50 -
minSupport  3 -i /user/hue/TweetsSeq /  -o /user/hue/TweetsVec -norm
2 -analyzerNamecom.packt.test.TweetsAnalyzer--sequentialAccessVector
```

In this command, the following terms represent:

- maxNGramSize: The maximum size of n-grams to be created
- minLLR: The minimum log likelihood ratio
- maxDFPercent: The maximum frequency of docs for document frequency
- sequentialAccessVector: The whether output vector should be sequentialAccessVectors

Launching the Mahout job on the cluster

Mahout has a script under the bin folder of the installation. Notice line 120 onwards of the following script:

```
# CLASSPATH initially contains $MAHOUT_CONF_DIR, or defaults to
$MAHOUT_HOME/src/conf
CLASSPATH=${CLASSPATH}:$MAHOUT_CONF_DIR

if [ "$MAHOUT_LOCAL" != "" ]; then
echo "MAHOUT_LOCAL is set, so we don't add HADOOP_CONF_DIR to
classpath."
```

```
    elif [ -n "$HADOOP_CONF_DIR"  ] ; then
    echo "MAHOUT_LOCAL is not set; adding HADOOP_CONF_DIR to
    classpath."
      CLASSPATH=${CLASSPATH}:$HADOOP_CONF_DIR
    fi
```

We can set `HADOOP_HOME` and `HADOOP_CONF_DIR` to launch the Mahout job (algorithm) on the Hadoop cluster.

Just before the algorithm command, set the two previously mentioned parameters using the `export` command:

`export  HADOOP_HOME=<ur hadoop location>`

`export HADOOP_CONF_DIR=$HADOOP_HOME/conf`

The Mahout launcher script helps to launch the job locally or on a cluster.

Performance tuning for the job

Closely investigating the Mahout job shows that Mahout jobs can create CPU and network bottlenecks. The distance computation and vectorization process is a CPU bound activity, while transmitting centroids to the reducer is a network bound activity. By closely investigating the parameters of the job's CPU, network, disk, and so on, the pitfalls can be avoided.

We can create a different type of vector representation of data in Mahout, such as dense vector, sparse vector, and so on As per the definition of the dense vector, it saves the zero for non-existing elements. So, if the data is very sparse, the dense vector will unnecessarily serialize the data and slow down the performance. So, in this case, it is better to use sparse vector representation for the data. For the sparse vector selection, also choose the implementation based on the distance measure. For example, Sequential Sparse Vector is best suited for the cosine distance measure because there is a need for element by element dot product.

In Mahout, under the Mahout-integration module, under the `org.apache.mahout.bechmark` package, there are utility classes to test whether the `benchmarking.Vector-Benchmarks.java` class can be used to know what type of vector can be selected by what type of distance measure.

To avoid bottlenecks in disk and network I/O, select the vector representation correctly. HDFS replication itself provides a reduction in I/O bottlenecks, as data is available on multiple nodes and the mappers and reducers can separately access this data.

Reducing the number of clusters provides less computation, and hence, better performance, but we can still reduce the number of clusters all the time, right? In batch processing, instead of dividing all the clusters into the first step, it is a good idea to use two level approaches. First, divide the data points into a smaller number of clusters that have more points each, and then further divide the clusters separately. But if new data points are expected, batch processing again will be a tedious task. A semi-online clustering technique can be achieved as follows (the steps are defined *Chapter 11* of *Mahout in Action*, *Sean Owen*, *Robin Anil*, *Ted Dunning*, and *Ellen Friedman*, *Manning*):

- Cluster the documents and save centroids of those clusters
- For new incoming documents, calculate the centroids using Canopy clustering and assign these to nearby centroids
- With a certain frequency rerun, the entire clustering process on all documents and recalculate the centroids

So, using the techniques discussed here, we can carry out performance tuning of the job, and with the underlying Hadoop cluster, we do not need to worry about the scalability.

Now, go back to our previously computed tweets and using analyzers, run the K-means clustering. Run the following command:

```
bin/mahoutkmeans --input /user/hue/TweetsVec--output
/user/hue/KmeansTweetout --clusters /user/hue/kmeanscenter --
numClusters 1000 --
distanceMeasureorg.apache.mahout.common.distance.CosineDistanceMeasur
e --maxIter 20 --method mapreduce --clustering
```

As previously mentioned, we can view the cluster using the following command:

```
bin/mahout  clusterdump -i /user/hue/KmeansTweetout/clusters-10 -o
/user/hue/tweetclusterdumpout.txt -d
/user/hue/TweetsVec/dictionary.file-0 -dtsequencefile --pointsDir
/user/hue/KmeansTweetout/clusteredPoints
```

Summary

In this chapter, you learned about the techniques used in the production environment. We discussed how to launch the Mahout job on the Hadoop cluster and how to look at some of the commonly occurring performance bottleneck issues. We took up a real-world use case to cluster similar Twitter users based on their tweets.

Now, you are ready to use Mahout in your production environment with real-world problems related to clustering.

Index

S

sequential algorithms 12
Silhouette coefficient
  about 23, 92
  URL 93
spectral clustering
  about 71
  affinity (similarity) graph 72
  graph Laplacian, obtaining from affinity
     matrix 73
  Mahout implementation 78-82
  uses 71
spectral clustering algorithm
  about 77
  normalized spectral clustering 78
  unnormalized spectral clustering 77
Stochastic Singular Value Decomposition
    (SSVD)
  about 82
  URL 82
Streaming K-means
  about 59, 60
  BallKMeans step 63
  CSV file, converting to vector file 65, 66
  dataset selection 64
  implementing 60
  Mahout, using 64
  running 66-68
  Streaming step 60-62
  URL 59
Streaming step
  about 60-62
  Beta parameter 62
  clusterLogFactor parameter 62
  clusterOvershoot parameter 62
  distanceCutOff parameter 62
  numClusters parameter 62
  URL 63

T

techniques, clustering
  about 10
  density-based method 12
  hierarchical methods 10
  partitioning method 11
  probabilistic clustering 12
TF-IDF 19
topic modeling 53
Twitter Apps
  URL 98
Twitter streams
  collecting, URL 96

W

Windows users
  setting up 17

Thank you for buying
Apache Mahout Clustering Designs

About Packt Publishing

Packt, pronounced 'packed', published its first book, *Mastering phpMyAdmin for Effective MySQL Management*, in April 2004, and subsequently continued to specialize in publishing highly focused books on specific technologies and solutions.

Our books and publications share the experiences of your fellow IT professionals in adapting and customizing today's systems, applications, and frameworks. Our solution-based books give you the knowledge and power to customize the software and technologies you're using to get the job done. Packt books are more specific and less general than the IT books you have seen in the past. Our unique business model allows us to bring you more focused information, giving you more of what you need to know, and less of what you don't.

Packt is a modern yet unique publishing company that focuses on producing quality, cutting-edge books for communities of developers, administrators, and newbies alike. For more information, please visit our website at www.packtpub.com.

About Packt Open Source

In 2010, Packt launched two new brands, Packt Open Source and Packt Enterprise, in order to continue its focus on specialization. This book is part of the Packt Open Source brand, home to books published on software built around open source licenses, and offering information to anybody from advanced developers to budding web designers. The Open Source brand also runs Packt's Open Source Royalty Scheme, by which Packt gives a royalty to each open source project about whose software a book is sold.

Writing for Packt

We welcome all inquiries from people who are interested in authoring. Book proposals should be sent to author@packtpub.com. If your book idea is still at an early stage and you would like to discuss it first before writing a formal book proposal, then please contact us; one of our commissioning editors will get in touch with you.

We're not just looking for published authors; if you have strong technical skills but no writing experience, our experienced editors can help you develop a writing career, or simply get some additional reward for your expertise.

Apache Mahout Cookbook

ISBN: 978-1-84951-802-4   Paperback: 250 pages

A fast, fresh, developer-oriented dive into the world of Apache Mahout

1. Learn how to set up a Mahout development environment.

2. Start testing Mahout in a standalone Hadoop cluster.

3. Learn to find stock market direction using logistic regression.

4. Over 35 recipes with real-world examples to help both skilled and the non-skilled developers get the hang of the different features of Mahout.

Learning Apache Mahout

ISBN: 978-1-78355-521-5   Paperback: 250 pages

Acquire practical skills in Big Data Analytics and explore data science with Apache Mahout

1. Learn to use Apache Mahout for Big Data Analytics.

2. Understand machine learning concepts and algorithms and their implementation in Mahout.

3. A comprehensive guide with numerous code examples and end-to-end case studies on Customer Analytics and Text Analytics.

Please check **www.PacktPub.com** for information on our titles

Apache Mahout Essentials

ISBN: 978-1-78355-499-7   Paperback: 164 pages

Implement top-notch machine learning algorithms for classification, clustering, and recommendations with Apache Mahout

1. Apply machine learning algorithms effectively in production environments with Apache Mahout.

2. Gain better insights into large, complex, and scalable datasets.

3. Fast-paced tutorial, covering the core concepts of Apache Mahout to implement machine learning on Big Data.

Learning Apache Mahout Classification

ISBN: 978-1-78355-495-9   Paperback: 130 pages

Build and personalize your own classifiers using Apache Mahout

1. Explore the different types of classification algorithms available in Apache Mahout.

2. Create and evaluate your own ready-to-use classification models using real world datasets.

3. A practical guide to problems faced in classification with concepts explained in an easy-to-understand manner.

Please check **www.PacktPub.com** for information on our titles